J. Du

A BISHOP'S MESSAGE

PHILADELPHIA
GEORGE W. JACOBS & COMPANY
PUBLISHERS

A BISHOP'S MESSAGE

Counsels on Some of the Manifold Problems
Confronting Clergymen To-day

BY THE
RIGHT REV. ETHELBERT TALBOT, D.D., LL.D.
BISHOP OF BETHLEHEM

PHILADELPHIA
GEORGE W. JACOBS & COMPANY
PUBLISHERS

TO

THE CLERGY WHOM I HAVE ORDAINED, AND MY
YOUNG MEN WHO ARE LOOKING FORWARD
TO THE SACRED MINISTRY, THIS BOOK
IS AFFECTIONATELY DEDICATED

PREFACE

The thoughts which have found expression in the following pages have occurred to the writer at various times during a ministry of over thirty years of which nearly all have been spent in the work and office of a Bishop in the Church of God.

In holding retreats and quiet hours with his Clergy, the author has frequently found occasion to counsel his younger brethren with reference to the cultivation of the spiritual life, the practical difficulties and dangers of the pastoral office, and many of the problems which confront the Clergyman in the discharge of his duties under the conditions of modern life.

He has also been permitted to have a share in guiding many young men in their studies and preparation for the Holy Ministry.

This book may therefore be regarded as literally the outgrowth of his varied experiences and many sided contacts with men in different stages of their religious life and development.

He offers no apology for imposing on the read-

PREFACE

ing public the results of his own observation, and hopes that this book may prove of some slight service, not only to his own younger Clergy, but to that larger constituency of ministers both within and beyond his own communion who may be interested in the subjects herein treated.

In deference to the oft repeated request of those who have heard many of these familiar talks, they would have long since been published had they not been delivered either extemporaneously or from the briefest notes.

To prepare them in their present form has been made possible only by utilizing the leisure hours of a few weeks vacation in which he has found time to arrange and marshal the material gathered through many years, and set it forth with some reference to a natural and logical sequence.

As his former book, " A Bishop Among His Flock," addressed to his Laity, has met with such indulgent and generous acceptance, the writer cherishes the hope that these counsels to his Clergy may likewise prove helpful and inspiring.

ETHELBERT TALBOT.

Bishop's House, South Bethlehem, Pa.

CONTENTS

CHAPTER		PAGE
I	A VALID CALL TO THE MINISTRY	11
II	THE FOOLISHNESS OF PREACHING	22
III	THE PARSON AND HIS DEVOTIONAL LIFE	35
IV	THE PARSON DEALING WITH SOULS	49
V	PARISH VISITING	61
VI	THE PARSON AS A BUSINESS MAN	74
VII	THE PARSON AS A CITIZEN	86
VIII	VARIOUS TYPES OF CHURCHMANSHIP	95
IX	THE PARSON AMONG HIS BOOKS	106
X	MAKING USE OF THE LAITY	118
XI	THE PARSON AS A MAN AMONG MEN	131
XII	THE PARSON AND HIS VESTRY	143
XIII	THE PARSON AND HIS CHOIR	154
XIV	THE PARSON AND HIS SUNDAY SCHOOL	169
XV	THE PARSON CONDUCTING PUBLIC WORSHIP	181
XVI	THE PARSON AND THE INSTITUTIONAL CHURCH	194
XVII	THE PARSON AND HIS DIOCESE	209

I

A VALID CALL TO THE MINISTRY

It may be well to ask in the beginning, "What constitutes a valid call to be a Minister of Christ?" The most obvious answer to this question is that a valid call is one in which the person concerned has been convinced that for him to consecrate himself to the service of his fellow-men in the work of preaching the Gospel, is in accordance with the will of God. Unless a man feels, after earnest and heart-searching prayer and a sincere effort to ascertain God's will, that such a vocation is in entire harmony with the divine purpose in his behalf, he may well hesitate to undertake it. It is in determining this vital and all important issue that so many fatal mistakes have been made.

In the case of St. Paul, that great Apostle could say, "Woe unto me if I preach not the

Gospel." So imperative had been the call which summoned him to his life work, he felt that to refuse would be to invite upon himself the severest condemnation. But in this instance all doubt and scruple had been removed by the fact that he had been the subject of a special and supernatural revelation direct from Christ Himself. The Master appeared unto him for that purpose. "To make him a minister" and a witness "to open the eyes of the Gentiles, and to turn them from darkness into light." With St. Paul it was simply a question of obedience to the unmistakable voice of the risen and ascended Christ. He declares, in recounting the scene, that he "was not disobedient to the heavenly vision." But this unique experience of the Apostle furnishes no model for us in these modern days who live under the ordinary dispensation of God's Providence. God's usual method of calling men today is that of appealing to their mind and conscience. But we are fallible in our judgments and liable to mistake our own weak and erring desires and opinions for a clear call to God.

A VALID CALL TO THE MINISTRY

It is reported that after an exciting period of a religious revival in which the emotions of the community were greatly stirred, a young man presented himself to the Presiding Elder of the Methodist Church and said he desired to become a Preacher. On being questioned by his ecclesiastical superior as to how he had arrived at that frame of mind, he replied that the night before he had seen in the sky, written in large characters of gold, the letters P. C.—Preach Christ. As the Presiding Elder knew the young man well, as a person very excitable, and otherwise utterly unfitted for the work of the Ministry, he said to him, " But, my young brother, you are mistaken. P. C. does not mean in your case, Preach Christ. It means Plow Corn. You will be doing God's will most truly if you continue to help your father on the farm."

To avoid such premature and unwise decisions, the Church has wisely ordained that what may be termed the inner call shall be authenticated and countersigned by the outward approval and judgment of others who are duly qualified to pass upon our moral and intellectual fitness for the work of the Ministry. Not every one who imagines himself called to this work is necessarily correct in his judgment. The young man is therefore wisely directed by the Church to lay before his Pastor his desire, and if encouraged by him, to proceed with his purpose; he is then to apply to his Bishop to become a Postulant for Holy Orders. Thus the responsibility for such an important decision affecting the life of the applicant as well as the spiritual interest of the Church, is shared at the very beginning by these two persons who would naturally be disposed to encourage any man whom they deemed worthy for such an important undertaking.

But this is not the only safeguard the Church employs. After the man has been accepted as a Postulant, and has passed the necessary examinations to qualify him for entrance upon a course of study in preparation for Holy Orders, he must apply to the Standing Committee of the Diocese to be admitted as a Candidate. Before he can be recognized as such, a Minister and

Vestry, who have personally known him for at least three years, or are fully possessed of evidence satisfactory to them that he is a fit person, must recommend him to the Bishop.   If accepted, he is then directed to enter upon his sacred studies under the direction of his Bishop for a period generally of at least three years.   Meanwhile his life and conversation are open to the inspection and approval of his superiors.

When his studies have been completed, and he is intellectually prepared for Ordination, the record of his life must again be carefully reviewed by the Standing Committee of the Diocese who must bear witness to his mental and moral fitness for the discharge of his sacred functions and the Bishop must again give his approval.

When one considers how many and technical are the precautionary measures taken to prevent any unworthy persons from being ordained, one wonders that any should be admitted who do not reflect credit upon the Church's Ministry.

However, this is only another proof of the weakness of our frail human nature, and when we realize that even among the twelve Apostles, chosen by our Lord Himself, there was one who proved a traitor and betrayed Him, we should not be surprised that errors of judgment are found among men to-day.

It is said that when Phillips Brooks consulted a Professor at Harvard as to what career he could most wisely devote himself, that good friend told him that whatever else he might be thinking of, it was quite evident he must lay aside all thought of the Ministry on account of his impediment of speech. It was not easy even for the Professor to discern in the stammering youth who consulted him one of the greatest orators and prophets of the Christian Church.

A venerable Missionary Bishop, well known to the writer, the late Bishop Morris of Oregon, after a long life spent in the Episcopate, was accustomed to remark that while he had ordained but few men to the Ministry, he thanked God that he had been instrumental in keeping many unworthy ones out.

Considering the unspeakably awful issues at

stake, both for the man himself, and for the souls to whom he would be called to minister, it is evident that too much care cannot be taken to lay hands suddenly on no man, but faithfully and wisely to make choice of fit persons to serve in the sacred Ministry of God's Church.

From time to time, of recent years, there has been a lamentable and somewhat alarming dearth of young men offering themselves for the work of the Ministry. Various causes for this have been suggested, such as the inadequate compensation of the Clergy, and the consequent life of hardship which they would be called upon to endure. Others have alleged that this falling off of candidates for the Ministry is an indication of decaying faith in the reality of spiritual things among us; while still others have asserted that the amazing and brilliant opportunities for success in commercial life, offered at the present day, have appealed to the imagination of our best young men and drawn them into the pursuit of money. There is no doubt that all of these causes, and others which might be mentioned, have operated to bring about a scarcity of the right material for this high and important office. But is it not at least conceivable that many of our most gifted and well disposed young men are hesitating about entering the ranks of the Clergy just because they fail to see in those already engaged in that work those high ideals of happy consecration and enthusiastic devotion, those marks of leadership and service among men which can only come as the result of choosing the best material? The surest way to increase the supply of the right kind of men is to improve the quality of those ordained. The contagion of a noble example in the Ministry, of a life touched with the fire of God's spirit, and filled with a passion for souls, and animated with a self-forgetful consecration to the service of his fellowmen, can hardly fail to instil in young men a like desire to serve.

There is no joy like the joy of the Ministry of Christ, but to enter into that joy demands the absolute surrender of a man to the will of the Master. One must lose himself in the love of

Christ to find himself in the atmosphere of an irresistible desire for unselfish service.

The demands upon the modern Minister, in the way of intellectual equipment, moral and spiritual culture, are far more exacting than in former years, and no shortcut to so great a responsibility ought to be encouraged. Far more important, however, than any knowledge which the schools can impart, is the possession of the spirit of devotion to one's fellowman, an utter willingness to serve him which can only come in answer to prayer.

There are three great words of the divine Master which might serve to test the validity of our call to the Ministry. They are words which connote three great spiritual principles which animated Him, and may well inspire any man looking forward to the Ministry. Those principles are a sense of Divine Companionship, a sense of personal mission, and a sense of the glory and moral beauty of service. Here they are. First, " I am not alone." He was stayed and comforted in all hours of doubt and discouragement by the assurance of His Father's presence. Secondly, " I have come not to do mine own will, but the will of Him that sent Me." This clear sense of a divine mission urged Him on always to the highest and best. It was this sense of mission that led St. Paul to say, " This one thing I do." Without this overmastering sense of a specific mission, a Minister's life may indeed be that of a member of a respectable profession, but it can never be a life of spiritual power. With this sense of mission clearly before him, he will have a passionate, definite, and triumphant motive ever present to inspire and nerve him to his best endeavor. Thirdly, " I am not come to be ministered unto, but to minister, and to give my life a ransom for many." So vital did our Lord consider this passion for service that He illustrated it to the great amazement of His Disciples by girding Himself and stooping down and condescending literally to wash the soiled feet of His Disciples.

There can be no highly successful and Christ-like Ministry without this glad willingness to serve our fellowmen. Following in the footsteps of his Master, the Minister of Christ can hesitate at no act of self-effacement, no exercise of patience, no persistency of love, that he may win those for whom the Saviour died, and whose souls are precious in His sight.

II

THE FOOLISHNESS OF PREACHING

As in St. Paul's day, even so now, it still pleases God " to save them that believe by the foolishness of preaching." Therefore the questions why shall I preach, what shall I preach, and how shall I preach, must always be invested with a vital interest to every earnest and conscientious minister of the Gospel.

And first of all, let us consider why shall I preach? How does it happen that preaching is still necessary? It is easy to understand why this method of propagating the faith was of prime importance at the beginning of the Christian era. Books were very scarce and expensive, the printing press, with its enormous power of disseminating knowledge by way of literature, magazines and newspapers, was unknown, and moreover, comparatively few of the people could read.

If the good news was to spread far and wide and reach all classes of men, such result could only be achieved by means of the living voice, bearing testimony to the faith that was in them.

Because of the greatly increased means of dissemination through other agencies, there are those who claim that the power of the pulpit in these modern days has waned, and that the office of the preacher at present is neither as necessary nor commanding as formerly. They assert that through the press all who desire to ascertain the truth can find it, and that while preaching may be a useful adjunct in imparting religious knowledge, men are no longer dependent on the pulpit for their inspiration and guidance.

But those who thus reason, leave out of consideration a fundamental element in human nature. It is that the message of our Christian faith cannot be written in a book, nor can it be displayed in some stately form of ritual. Books, and especially the Book of Books, are important. An impressive and dignified ceremonial may well accompany and symbolize a living faith. But the

faith itself must be embodied in a life and communicated by a living person. It can only find
adequate expression in terms of personality.
This personal testimony of the Disciple who has
caught the mood and genius and spirit of the
Master is the only abiding method of imparting
it. By the subtle irresistible power of spiritual
contagion, the message must be passed on by
those who have personally felt its effect. Many
words are made print, but "the Word" which
saves the world is made flesh, and dwells among
us, full of grace and truth.

Therefore, as long as human nature remains
what it is, the time will never come when the
necessity for the preacher and prophet of God
is not paramount. Indeed the greater the increase of knowledge and intelligence on every
hand, and the more widespread the education of
the people, all the more will there be a demand
for the well-equipped and consecrated priest of
God to interpret to the age the divine message.

St. Paul asks, "How shall they hear without
a preacher, and how shall they preach except they

be sent?" We who are called to this high and sacred privilege cannot therefore be too profoundly impressed with the tremendous importance of the dignity and necessity of preaching. Unto us, God has committed the word of reconciliation. We are ambassadors for Christ, as though God did beseech men by us to be reconciled to Him.

Other duties of the Christian ministry, it need hardly be urged, are also important. There is the reverent esteem of the holy sacraments as channels for the conveyance of divine grace and their worthy celebration; there is pastoral visiting, and the ministering to individual souls; more especially, there is the care of the sick and the relief of the poor; but it is no disparagement of any of these, if we give jealous heed to preaching and carefully safeguard it against any infringement or loss of power. That minister alone can hope for the greatest blessing of God in winning souls who holds in high esteem the dignity of " rightly dividing the word of God."

We cannot all be pulpit orators, but it is possible for every clergyman to bring to the work of preaching a spirit which will lead him to consecrate his best gifts of mind and heart towards its greatest efficiency.

We are now ready to ask the question: What shall I preach? If we thus appreciate the vital importance of preaching as here set forth, and lay the proper emphasis upon it in the plan of redemption, we should have no great difficulty in deciding what to preach. We read that the great apostle to the Gentiles preached, " Jesus and the Resurrection"; again that he preached " Christ crucified." Interpreting these two striking phrases broadly, and bearing in mind that the mission of Christianity is to bring the life and power and example of the Master home to the heart of the individual, we have before us a sufficiently definite and inspiring aim. Every message delivered in the name and under the authority of Jesus Christ should be filled with His spirit.

Even though the sacred name of Christ should not be mentioned in our sermon, yet it ought to be manifest to those who hear it, that the preacher has been inspired and guided by the mind and temper of the Master. It ought not to be possible for any intelligent critic in fairness to make the charge that our utterance is out of harmony with the divine will as interpreted and exemplified by the life and teaching of Christ. If we are sure that the aspect of truth, which we desire to emphasize, has behind it the unmistakable approval of our Lord, we shall be emboldened to declare it with all the power that springs from such a conviction.

There is no question which may arise in the life of the individual, the community, or the nation, which cannot be interpreted in the light of the Gospel. Christianity is a message for the guidance of human life under all its manifold conditions, and the preacher who has caught the genius and spirit of the Saviour of men, will know how to make the application. All life, whether individual, social, commercial, political, or national, is related to Him and is to be judged by His spirit. The eternal Christ of yesterday, to-day, and forever, is as truly guiding and teaching His Church to-day as when He trod these earthly courts, and it is the province of a vital Christianity to so modernize and adapt the ever fresh and potent faith, once for all delivered to the saints as to make its influence felt in the lives of men.

There has never been a time when men were more responsive to the appeal of Christ than the present, and the world is eager to catch the echo of His commanding voice as His prophet sounds it forth amid the conflicting counsels of men.

There is therefore, to-day, the largest opportunity for the ambassador of Christ, equipped with the regenerating influence of the spirit, to make His impress on the age, and to contribute his share towards the bringing in of the Kingdom of Righteousness. There is practically no limitation to the freedom of the preacher's choice of a theme, for nothing is foreign to the Gospel message which has for its object the promotion of right relations between God and man, and the ushering in of the reign of universal brotherhood and good-will.

As to the question, how shall I preach, we may well regard it as secondary. Assuming that a minister of Christ has anything like an adequate motive for preaching, and an intelligent conception of its great theme, as revealed in the breadth and length, and depth and height of the love of Christ, we need not long dwell on the method of delivering the message.

And yet while one's method of giving expression to the truth as compared with its supreme motive, and the subject matter of that truth, may seem unimportant, we are far from saying that it ought to be despised. Shall the sermon be delivered with or without notes? To this question we should be disposed to reply, adopt that method which in each individual case will prove most effective. No iron-clad and invariable rule can be laid down which is equally applicable to every individual.

There are those who are possessed of such temperament as to make it possible, without great effort, to cultivate the habit of ready and effective expression, even though it be not natural to them. There are others who, even by the putting forth of the most patient and strenuous endeavor, can never achieve any facility of public utterance without the aid of their manuscript.

It may perhaps be conceded that where the power has been thoroughly acquired, a message delivered without notes is likely to prove at once more pleasing and telling. Such a method enables the preacher to lay under tribute and bring into service whatever aids to persuasion may come from the free use of the body, and especially the eye and countenance. It is the more natural method of speaking when a man is profoundly in earnest and greatly moved. At the same time some of the greatest preachers of our own, or any age, have been men who achieved their reputation by confining themselves entirely to the written page. Such was the practice of Canon Liddon, and of our own Phillips Brooks, save in the latter part of his remarkable career.

THE FOOLISHNESS OF PREACHING

It is possible, in some instances, to acquire such familiarity with the manuscript, and such freedom and facility in making use of it, that a congregation would find it difficult to determine whether the sermon was being read or spoken entirely without the aid of notes.

Whatever method of delivery is adopted, it will be admitted that there ought always to be something worth delivering. In other words, a man should have a message for the people, and it should be thoroughly prepared. The truth to be brought home to his hearers should have so possessed, not only the mind, but the heart of the preacher, as to leave no doubt with those who hear him, that he is deeply in earnest, and feels that what he has to say is worthy of their best consideration. The man must be behind the message. Strictly speaking, no man can persuade others, who is not himself first persuaded, and while a man must preach the Gospel, it must be the Gospel as experienced and interpreted by his own life.

Given a man, whose soul is afire with his message, and whose life is consecrated to the privilege of communicating it to his brother-man, we may well leave the details of manner and method to the individual. It is quite customary at the present day for many of our young men to pride themselves on their ability to dispense with manuscript. They call themselves extempore speakers. If by this phrase they mean that they have trained themselves, after most careful preparation of their subject matter, to present their message in a clear, thoughtful, orderly and persuasive manner without their notes, let us congratulate them by all means. But if they mean simply, that whatever they have to say, whether prepared or unprepared, they propose to deliver it without any help from the written page, such a practice may lead to fatal results. There is a fluency that borders close upon flippancy, and the young preacher must be on his guard against cultivating, as a substitute for well digested, wholesome food, the blatant vapors of meaningless words.

It is well to gain such self-mastery as to enable a man to rise to his feet and express himself intelligently and well whenever called upon. That kind of ability is well worth our best efforts. But let us beware of depending on mere facility of utterance, for the temptation is an insidious one and grows stronger with indulgence. The best preparation for a sermon is in the heart of the preacher, and if he brings to the pulpit a message steeped with a noble purpose of helping his brother-man, some effective way of communicating it is sure to be found.

Irrespective of methods of preaching, the habit of carefully writing out our sermons should not be neglected. It is Lord Bacon who says that writing makes the accurate man, reading the full man, and speaking the ready man. Not Lord Bacon only, but all thoughtful men will testify to the truth of this pregnant statement, and it may also be added that the highest proficiency in public speaking cannot be achieved without paying the price of conscientious and painstaking effort. If much writing gives accuracy of thought and clearness of expression, much reading, especially of our Bible, the preacher's great storehouse and armory, supplemented by the mastery of other great books, will supply that fullness of knowledge out of which readiness of well ordered speech will the more persuasively flow.

III

THE PARSON AND HIS DEVOTIONAL LIFE

" The life is more than meat and the body than raiment."   Above all knowledge, wisdom, power, eloquence, emphasis is here placed by our Divine Master on the kind of life a man leads.   What a parson is in the sight of God counts far more than what he says or does.   " Do not speak to me," said Emerson, with a pardonable exaggeration, " what you are thunders so loud, that I cannot hear what you say." Nothing would be easier than to multiply illustrations to show that to-day, in this twentieth century, as of old, the life is the light of men.   Indeed, sooner or later it will be found that the influence which proceeds from the conviction that the parson is above all things a sincere and humble man of God, whose heart is set on doing His will, makes every sermon a message of help and comfort, and every outward act an inspiration to his flock. And conversely, though he speaks with the " tongues of men and of angels," and has a faith that can remove mountains, yet if he be lacking in Godliness, that bond of peace and of all virtues, he is as nothing. Even before the imagination of St. Paul there loomed up the terrible possibility lest, that having preached to others, he himself might be a castaway.

That he may be used by the Holy Spirit as an instrument to save the souls of his brother men, it is vitally necessary that the parson's own soul shall first be saved.

At that most solemn moment in a parson's life, when he stands before the Bishop and in the presence of the congregation is examined as to his mind and will in seeking the ministry of reconciliation, this question is addressed to him, " Will you apply your diligence to frame and fashion your own life and the life of your family according to the doctrine of Christ and to make both yourself and them as much as lieth in you, wholesome examples to the flock of

Christ?" The act of Ordination would be worse than a mockery were it to fail to lay emphasis at that critical hour on that which is the prime condition of an acceptable service, namely, a heart devoted to the love of God and a life agreeable to His holy will. Herein the joy of the Ministry, its highest compensations, all its most worthy inspiration, its abiding support and its sole justification consist. In all our thoughts and activities, in all our plans and ambitions, care must be taken that Christ and not ourselves shall have the pre-eminence.

Probably there never was an age in the whole history of the Church when this note of personal consecration, or holiness in the minister of Christ counted so much. At the same time it must be confessed that the conditions of modern life are not such as to make the cultivation of spirituality on the part of the parson an easy achievement. Opportunity for personal service on every side is abundant and manifold. Many worthy objects of parochial activity make demands on his time and tend to divert his attention from the more quiet and contemplative side of life. Interesting problems of a social, charitable or educational character clamor for solution and press upon the busy days of the active Clergyman and threaten to fill up every hour with their incessant demands.

Unless the parson first of all realizes the prime importance of constantly refreshing his own soul from the inexhaustible storehouse of God's bounty, no progress will be made. At whatever cost to his own ease and comfort, moreover, he must jealously provide a time and place for his own spiritual enrichment and daily communings with God in prayer. If it is entirely true that *laborare est orare,* it is also equally true that to pray is to work, and under present day surroundings really to pray demands hard and painstaking and persistent labor.

And first as to the times or hours which should find the parson on his knees. His private devotions must be regulated by himself, and should in a measure at least be governed by circumstances. Far more important than the hours set apart for that holy exercise, is the strictness and regularity with which they are observed. Time redeemed in the quiet of the early morning, when the mind and body have been refreshed by sleep has been found, in the experience of holy men, most conducive to devotion. There can be no more fitting way in which to begin the duties of the day. Then the noonday hour when our Lord hung upon the cross stretching forth His loving arms for our redemption, is another time when perhaps even the busiest parson will find delight in withdrawing to the privacy of his closet and making a brief intercession for the spread of God's Kingdom. Again when the labors of the day are over, what is more in harmony with the dictates of a grateful spirit than an offering of praise and thanksgiving for the blessings vouchsafed us and commending ourselves to God's holy keeping during the hours of darkness. Of course those hours called canonical will naturally and properly be observed by those who are living in a religious community. But our chief contention now is that the parson, under any and all circumstances, should keep with fixed regularity his times of prayer and meditation, when he can be literally alone with God and realize His presence.

When the first Bishop of New Zealand, the great Selwyn, was one day sitting in his study a knock was heard at the door. It was one of his native catechists from a far distant station. "Why have you come?" enquired the Bishop. "I want to be filled up and the people tell me I need to be filled up," was the man's reply. How truly the parson might make the same confession himself. He is so constantly giving out that he is in danger of becoming spiritually exhausted. It is ever more life and fuller that he needs. How is he to get it save by prayer and communion with God? He must realize his entire dependence upon the divine supply to satisfy his craving for help and guidance. He must come to the source of power deeply conscious of his own unworthiness and insufficiency. That is the prime condition, the first necessity. Said the late Bishop Wilberforce of Winchester, " Whilst we may find instances of great success in the Ministry of those who have lacked almost every other qualification, there can, I believe, be no instances found of a successful ministry which was not full of prayers." Some of you have read the story of the Vicar in a village where the Church stands on the summit of a considerable hill. When the nights are dark and the wind is rising, it has long been his practice to go up to the Church and kindle the beacon light on the tower as a guide to the simple fishermen who are tossed upon the angry waves. They see the light as it flashes over the waters and they know that their good parson is spending the intervals of the night in the Church at prayer for their souls and their bodies. We need not wonder that they love him with a great devotion and are ready to spend and be spent for him in return. The following extract from William Laws's great classic, "The Serious Call," shows the effect of a habit of devout and earnest prayer upon both the worker and the work. "Ouranius is a holy priest, full of the spirit of the Gospel, watching, laboring and praying for a poor country village. Every soul in it is as dear to him as himself; and he loves them all as he loves himself; because he prays for them all as often as he prays for himself. It would strangely delight you with what spirit he converses, with what tenderness he reproves, with what affection he exhorts and with what vigor he preaches; and it is all owing to this, because he reproves, exhorts, and preaches to those for whom he first prays to God. This devotion softens his heart, enlightens his mind, sweetens his temper, and makes everything that comes from him, instructive, amiable and affecting.

" At his first coming to this little village it was as disagreeable to him as a prison, and every day seemed too tedious to be endured in so retired a place. He thought his Parish was too full of poor and common people, that they were not fit for the conversation of a gentleman. This was his polite, or I may rather say, poor ignorant turn of mind, before devotion had got the government of his heart. But now his days are so far from being tedious, or his parish too great a retirement that he now only wants more time to do that variety of good which his soul thirsts after. The solitude of his little parish is become a matter of great comfort to him because he hopes that God has placed him and his flock there to make it their way to heaven.

" He can now not only converse with but gladly attend and wait upon the poorest kind of people. He is now daily watching over the weak, and infirm, humbling himself to perverse rude and ignorant people, wherever he can find them; and so far from desiring to be considered as a gentleman, that he desires to be used as the servant of all; and in the spirit of his Lord and Master, girds himself, and is glad to kneel down and wash any of their feet.

" All these noble thoughts and divine sentiments are the effects of his great devotion; he presents every one so often before God in his prayers, that he never thinks he can esteem, reverence or serve those enough, for whom he implores so many mercies from God.

" These are the happy effects which a devout intercession has produced in the life of Ouranius."

In such a spirit and life of prayer, believe me, lies the real secret of influence. It does not consist in a copying of what is most noticeable in the lives and actions of other men; still less does it depend upon external conditions of station, material strength, or wealth. Indeed, money and earthly resources may even be detrimental when it is a question of exerting the influence which is to do most for the upbuilding of the life of God in man. It is recorded that Innocent IV and Thomas Aquinas were standing together as the bags of treasure were being carried in through the gates of the Lateran. " You see," observed the Pope, with a smile, " the day is past when the Church could say, ' silver and gold have I none.' " " Yes, Holy Father," was the Saint's reply, " and the day is past also when the Church could say to the lame man, ' Rise and walk.' "

It is entirely right and proper that the parson should wish to be highly successful, and discharge his priestly functions acceptably to God. In striving for the mastery, he is tempted to imagine that intellectual gifts count for a great deal in the matter of such influence. Beyond question, they do, and yet it is even more certain, that they are not the chief factor, nor even an indispensable factor. The most learned and able have not seldom been those who have most conspicuously failed.

Again there can be no doubt that methods of organization may be made extremely effective; yet even these have a tendency to become fatally mechanical and the apparatus of machinery may be kept going for its own sake rather than for any spiritual good resulting from it. Neither will hard work accomplish everything, as is so often supposed. That is a sad illusion. All these gifts and activities have their place, but in the last analysis only one thing is needful, and that is a deep personal, childlike devotion to our Divine Master. That we may cherish that devotion, that we may love our Master with that consuming passion which alone will make His

service perfect freedom, and permanently mold
and influence our lives, we must learn to know
Him as He is. This intimate knowledge of Him
can best be acquired by living with Him during
the years in which He sojourned among men.
Our devotion will be quickened and stimulated
by placing ourselves in His company; by reverently and consciously associating ourselves with
Him as He reveals Himself to us in the pages of
the four Gospels.

We live in an age of books. There are numerous books of devotion, books of criticism, books
about the Gospels. But what amount of time
and careful, systematic study and labor do we
give to the Gospels themselves? How many of
us really live in the hallowing atmosphere of those
four wonderful Biographies? How many of us
so read, mark, learn and inwardly digest those
words and acts and scenes of our Lord's earthly
life, that we are led to embrace and ever hold fast
the blessed hope we find in our Lord Jesus Christ?

In these photographs of our great exemplar
we have pictures of what He was, taken from

four very different points of view. Thus His deeds, His words, His very looks become extraordinarily vivid and real to us. As a great Christian scholar has expressed it, " These writings bring back to you the living image of the most holy mind, the very Christ Himself speaking, healing, dying, rising, in fact so entirely present that you would see less of Him if you actually beheld Him with your eyes."

Let us set our gaze upon Him who is full of grace and truth. In Him only shall we behold the perfect ideal of beauty. In His fullness alone can we hope to discover what our own particular life was intended to be. Let us study to know more and more what He was like. Let us be filled with His spirit so that we may in ever so small a degree set forth the lineaments of His perfect manhood.

It is when the truth is brought home to us that we have a strictly personal interest and share in the great facts of the divine redemption that we are able to appropriate their value and force in such a degree as to make them the joy and inspiration of our lives. Is it not one great purpose of the sacraments to bring home to our hearts and minds our personal interest in Him? Who has not in some supreme moment of his life been thrilled and stirred by the words, " The Body of our Lord Jesus Christ which was given for thee? " Let us not forget as some one has so well said, that meditation on Him, prayer to Him, learning of Him, conformity to Him, partaking of Him, are the chief business of the Christian life.

CHAPTER IV

THE PARSON DEALING WITH SOULS

We now approach that which is at once the most responsible and at the same time the most delicate and difficult part of the parson's sacred vocation. He is a messenger, a watchman, and a steward of the Lord. With all due authority he has been commissioned by Christ Himself to teach, to premonish, to feed and provide for the Lord's family; He is to seek for Christ's sheep that are scattered abroad and for His children who are in the midst of this sinful world that they may be saved through Christ forever. He is to give such an account of every soul committed to him, that he may do it with joy and not with grief.

As the parson stands before the Bishop at the solemn hour of his Ordination, he is reminded of the greatness of the fault and the horrible punishment that will ensue, if it shall happen that

49

any member of his congregation take any hurt or hindrance by reason of his negligence. As he weighs with himself such a responsibility the most courageous man may well hesitate and with fear and trembling exclaim, " Who is sufficient for these things?" Surely nothing less than the grace of God, no power but the gift of the Holy Ghost, pledged and conveyed to him abundantly by prayer and the laying on of hands in answer to his faith would embolden him to undertake such a task. He is solemnly admonished and he knows in his own heart that he cannot have a mind and will to perform so great a work of himself but that the ability is given of God alone.

Three things stand out conspicuously in the service of Ordination. First, that the parson's great and absorbing work is to compass the salvation of the souls of his people. He seeks not theirs but them. Secondly, he is reminded of his sole dependence on the grace of God for the ability to perform his work. In the third place, he is assured of the presence and power of Jesus Christ vouchsafed him in the laying on of hands.

It only remains for him to stir up the grace of God thus given him.

Thus commissioned by the great head of the Church, and thus equipped with the manifold grace of the Holy Spirit, the newly ordained parson is sent to his appointed field of labor. How interesting and diversified his mission! He is to arouse the careless, the indifferent, the irreligious and profane. He is to inspire to greater zeal and good works all professed Christians. He is to make the acquaintance of the young people of his flock, the boys and girls that he may win them to Christ. He is to seek out the sick and aged, that he may cheer and comfort and minister to them. He is as yet a stranger in the community and has come to make his abode there and to identify himself with the life of his people. For the sake of his influence for good, he desires to secure the respect and esteem of all with whom he is brought into contact. He is glad to know personally all the people among whom he is about to make his home, whether they belong to his own congregation or not. As he is polite and courteous in his bearing and wishes to make friends, he finds a readiness on the part of the business men and others to greet him as he passes them on the street.

He realizes that while his public ministrations at the altar and in the pulpit count for much, his personal contact with individuals will afford him even greater opportunity of doing good. He knows that unless he can in some way win the confidence of his flock, and thus encourage them to express their views and opinions, their doubts and difficulties, much of his preaching will be a vain beating of the air and dwelling upon imaginary needs quite remote from their actual spiritual condition. To dispense the medicines of the Gospel as a good physician of souls, the parson must know something of the diseases with which the members of his congregation are troubled. In his rounds of Parish visiting he has found a young man whose faith, somewhat impaired by an infidel publication, needs to be strengthened. He has met a woman whose life has been sadly embittered by dwelling upon some real or imaginary wrong received long ago. He has found another parishioner who has been led to doubt God's love because of the sorrows which have come into his life. For all these and many other individual cases, he will have some helpful word which carries with it unspeakable comfort when most needed. In dealing with souls the parson will sometimes find it a slow and difficult task to secure such confidence as may enable him either personally or in his sermons to meet the special need.

While habitual and auricular confession does not seem in harmony with the genius and spirit of our prayer-book teaching, yet ample provision is made for those instances where souls, being unable to quiet their own consciences otherwise, but require further comfort or counsel, are exhorted to come to their own or some other minister of God's word and open their grief, that they may receive such Godly counsel and advice as they may require. Such confession of sins to one's minister and the receiving of that

comfort and grace of absolution thereby provided by the Church, might well be more frequently made use of than it is. The abuse of
private confession and the fact that it has in some
other communions been made compulsory should
not be allowed to deprive souls who need it of
its legitimate use as a purely voluntary act of
spiritual benefit. Indeed the mere fact that confession has been so generally practiced historically for so many years by great sections of the
Church Catholic, would lead us to regard with
favor the advice of our prayer-book in recom-
mending its use as a medicine when the need of
it is felt. But whatever may be the attitude and
practice of the parson in encouraging his people
to make use of the liberty which the Church
gives them in this regard, we may be sure that
unless they do repose in him such confidence as
to lead them to open their hearts to him and seek
counsel and help, his relations with them are not
such as they ought to be. A very devout and
prominent Presbyterian minister once remarked
to the writer, that he believed he heard more con-

fessions than all the other ministers in his town combined. This was simply another way of saying that his people brought to him in loving confidence their spiritual doubts, sorrows and difficulties and sought his help and guidance. Such close and intimate spiritual relationship must in some way find expression in the pastoral life and experience of every truly helpful minister of Christ.

In this sacred responsibility of dealing with souls, the faithful parson will find certain times and occasions most helpful. Among these may be mentioned visitations of death in the family when hearts ordinarily indifferent to the claims of religion become tender and susceptible and turn almost instinctively to God for help and comfort. Not infrequently a birth in a family predisposes the parents with grateful hearts to think of their duty to God. But no more favorable opportunity to mold and influence and deeply impress the spiritual life is presented in the ordinary course of parochial work than that of preparing an individual for confirmation. We speak of the individual rather than of the class although we are well aware that this work of preparation is, alas, too often done in a very superficial and perfunctory way. It is when this critical period is allowed to pass without dealing with the soul individually that a great wrong is perpetrated and a unique opportunity lost to permanently inform the mind and impress the heart with the great reality of things eternal. While much instruction may well be imparted by confirmation lectures addressed to classes or groups of candidates, that method should rather supplement than take the place of the personal heart to heart examination. We owe it to a person about to be confirmed to challenge his motives and aims and ideals and this can only be accomplished by the prayerful and conscientious effort of the parson as he deals with the individual alone. When a person, young or old, presents himself for confirmation, the parson has a right to assume that he desires to consecrate himself to the glad and loyal service of Christ. What that service involves should then be clearly and searchingly brought home to the heart and intelligence

56

of the candidate. The sacredness and solemnity of that contract between Christ and the individual then entered upon should be set forth with unmistakable clearness, in detail. Confirmation is the Church's ordained sacramental rite which admits a person to the privilege of the Holy Communion and the full responsibilities and privileges of the Christian life. If this is true then what kind of a life should a confirmed person lead? To say the least, it is a life in which a relationship of personal love and loyalty and obedience to Jesus Christ as God and Saviour has been established. The implications of this personal devotion to Christ should not be a vague, indefinite sentiment carrying with it no practical obligations and duties. There is first of all the great privilege of partaking of Christ in the blessed Sacrament, not as an occasional act, but as the Church provides, regularly and at least on every Lord's day when possible, and this should be laid upon the conscience, not so much as a duty, but as it is, a great and unspeakable joy, graciously provided for the soul's refreshment and

Heavenly food. Then there is the accompanying call and challenge to a life agreeable to such a communion and fellowship with Christ. It is because the parson fails to instruct the candidate for confirmation as to the nature of the Church as a divine institution with its three-fold ministry, its sacramental life, and its worship that our Church people are often so weak in the faith and so slack in their obedience and careless in their lives. Too often the parson utterly overlooks the fact that the candidate will be surrounded by many other forms of organized religion or Churches of many names. The distinctive doctrines of the Church of which the candidate is about to become an accredited communicant, her customs, historical lineage, her ministry, discipline and worship are frequently but lightly dwelt upon. As a result, the person when confirmed can give no worthy reason for the faith which is in him. He is not only sadly ignorant of the origin, teaching and practice of other religious bodies and of the Church's relation to them, but he is left hopelessly in the dark

58

as to what the teaching of his own communion really is. The questions as to how a lawful minister of Christ becomes such, what constitutes a valid sacrament, what is the meaning of the Church's various forms and customs and liturgy, how his Church differs fundamentally from the other Christian bodies surrounding her, these are left untouched. One person well and thoroughly instructed and thereby made capable of bearing an intelligent witness and testimony to others, is worth a score of ill informed and superficial candidates admitted to the communion without any adequate knowledge of the Church's ways. Such persons become a source of weakness if not a scandal to the Church, and are easily led astray and often disappear from the ranks of the faithful. Such sad betrayal of a trust imposed can often be traced directly to the parson himself who has simply failed to discharge a bounden duty at a time when the Church expects him to admit no one to her privileges who is not both ready and prepared.

The parson must realize above all things that

the divine method of propagating the faith and inspiring souls to the love of God is that of personality. The message must be embodied in a life. It can only find adequate expression as by the contagion of one person it is communicated to another. Moreover, this is the only abiding method. Innumerable good words have found their way into books, but The Word which saves the world is made flesh and dwells among us full of grace and truth.

The parson should try to cultivate a loving patience that never despairs of winning a soul however tempted and sinful. He should cherish a hopefulness born of the love wherewith Christ hath loved us and a spirit of humble thankfulness to God for calling him into the Ministry. He will rejoice at every manifestation of the Divine Presence and thus cheerfully accomplish the work committed to him. His disappointments will be many but amid them all his compensations will be those which unfailingly come to the man who has the joy of proclaiming in his life the unsearchable riches of Christ.

V

PARISH VISITING

The parable of the Good Shepherd, interpreted in the light of present day conditions, describes in a very picturesque way the ideal relation between a clergyman and his flock. The pastor has entered into his sheep-fold by the door, and is a real shepherd of the sheep. They gladly hear his voice which has become dear and familiar to them. He calls each one by his name, knowing them one by one, and even the little lambs are precious in his sight. He leads them forth into the green pastures of refreshment, and they delight to follow his guidance, for they know his voice and confide in his loving care.

He leads them, and does not attempt to drive them. They follow him, for he is no longer a stranger, but a true and well-tried friend. He is no hireling, doing so much work for so much pay, but really loves his sheep for what they are, and not for what they have and can give him. His heart has been moved to serve them in order that he may give them life and give it them more abundantly because he carries each one of them with his hopes and fears in his heart. Through many an experience of joy and sorrow in their homes, they have learned that their shepherd seeks not theirs but them; that he is waiting for their souls as one that must give an account, that he may do it with joy and not with grief. It is perfectly evident to the flock that their shepherd stands ready at all times to spend and to be spent in behalf of his flock, and even to lay down his life for them.

Animated by the spirit of such a relationship as that described by our Lord in this striking parable, let us now approach the discussion of the value of that feature of the pastor's work commonly understood by the term parish visiting.

At the very beginning let us frankly admit that the whole subject is attended by certain obvious difficulties. It is not unusual to find clergymen to whom much parish visiting seems a sheer and lamentable waste. Theoretically, it is easy enough to prove that it is the clear duty of our people to come to Church, and to faithfully discharge their Christian obligations without depending on their Rector to keep up their interest by constantly calling upon them. If Christian people were invariably governed by the highest principles of loyalty and devotion, it would be entirely safe for a minister to dispense with the formality of calling. In that case they would neither expect it, nor would their spiritual welfare demand it.

But as human nature is at present, and always has been constituted, who does not know that such ideal church members are the rare exceptions, and by no means the usual type. The personal touch between the shepherd and the individual sheep is absolutely necessary in the great majority of instances to keep our people keyed up to anything like a genuine and keen interest in the life and work of the parish. It has been found that their zeal will grow cool, and their enthusiasm slacken, if the only relation between themselves and their minister is a purely official one, in which they see him only in church, when he is leading their devotions, or on those infrequent occasions when they call upon him to celebrate a marriage, Baptism or funeral. In those branches of the historic church where auricular confession is the rule, such as the Roman and Greek Communions, the need of house to house visiting may not be so obvious. But with us among whom such confession is as yet voluntary and exceptional, and not the rule, there is no other way of maintaining the close personal relationship so necessary to create a vital and wholesome contact with things spiritual. Therefore, the familiar aphorism, that a house-going parson makes a church-going congregation, contains a truth that we cannot ignore save at the peril of our success.

No eloquence in the pulpit, or attractive power of our public ministrations, or even the charm and inspiration of the best music, can take the place of knowing our people in their homes. On the other hand, again and again, do we see instances where a very mediocre ability in the preacher, and an exceedingly unattractive service have not been sufficient to keep the people away where they have learned to love their pastor because he has first loved them, and has evinced that love by an individual and personal interest in them as their friend. His church has been filled Sunday after Sunday, by glad and devout worshipers, attracted by the bond of reverent affection, cemented by the faithful use of pastoral oversight.

To this insistence on parish visiting, it may with some truth be objected that the modern parish, with its busy parish house and its institutional work, its numerous guilds and brotherhoods of men and boys, its woman's auxiliaries and other missionary societies, leaves little or no time for such visiting. In all that we have thus far said, we have had in mind, and kept steadily before us, the conditions that prevail, even in the largest parish. But we still maintain that time must be systematically found for careful and thorough parish visiting whether the parish be large or small.

It is the peculiar glory of the modern parish, if it be really spiritually alive, that the doors of the church are always open, and that frequent, if not daily celebrations of the holy communion, and morning and evening prayer, as contemplated by the prayer-book, shall be offered. Where the parish is small, it will hardly be claimed that time cannot be found for such pastoral work, and in large parishes, curates are employed to assist the Rector in the various parochial activities, and especially in calling on people. But no wise rector will relegate to his curates, however acceptable they may be, the whole duty of pastoral visitation. The people who are likely to be neglected are the poor, the indifferent, and the non-churchgoers, and they are just the people who most need to feel that the rector himself cares for them and desires their interest and coöperation.

Therefore in making out the parish list for calls, it would be well to assign to the curate, the rich and comfortable and socially attractive.

PARISH VISITING

By all means let the rector reserve for himself, so far as he can, the Lord's poor and needy, and let him identify himself strongly with the common people, the rank and file of his flock. He will thus spare himself the stigma of being thought a snob and toady and at the same time will win the reverence of rich and poor alike. It is exceedingly important that the minister of Christ should cultivate in himself and others the spirit of a true and manly democracy, and make the people realize that as a clergyman, he cherishes for all of his flock, quite irrespective of their worldly circumstances, a profound reverence and consideration.

If we seem to lay special emphasis on the importance of parish visiting, it is simply because of the fact that for his highest influence, the minister must be known by his people, and what is of equal importance perhaps, he must know them; and it is only in the intimate and unrestrained life and atmosphere of the home that he can learn to know them well. This is especially true of the men, who for the most part can only be found at home with their families in the evening, owing to the exacting demands of their business.

The clergyman will also find frequent opportunities to drop in upon the men at their places of employment during their less busy hours. A brief call at such a time is often appreciated, and helps to familiarize him with the conditions of life and work among his parishioners, and to strengthen the bonds of sympathy between himself and them.

Clergymen to whom parish visiting is especially distasteful sometimes ask, " What shall we talk about when we do call? " We should be inclined to answer not necessarily about religion or the parish. It may well happen that it will be easier to interest the family by dwelling on their domestic or business affairs. Indeed as the object of the call is to become well acquainted with the household in order to serve them spiritually the clergyman should try and make himself agreeable and welcome to them and thus encourage them to give him their confidence. As in everything else in this world, a little tact and common sense should be exercised, and where these qualities do not come naturally to a man, he should try to cultivate them. Cheerfulness, absolute courtesy, and brevity, are three elements that ought to enter into the problem in every case, and also the use of some discrimination as to when the call can be most wisely made. There is no reason why such a visit should degenerate into a mere formality nor that a minister should forget his sacred office. But on the other hand, it is just as well for him to remember that his great desire is to sustain or quicken an interest in spiritual things. To this result, the brief call can gradually lead up. If we can secure the esteem and confidence of our people, and let them see that we really care for their highest and best interests, the chief difficulty will have been overcome.

Thus far, we have not dwelt upon the pastoral ministration to those, who, by reason of old age, are confined to their homes, and to visiting the sick, and those bereaved or in trouble. In all such cases an opportunity is given to show that gentleness and tender sympathy which open the way to a word of prayer and the consolations of religion. The baptism of every child, the celebration of every marriage, the occasion of every funeral, all these furnish opportunities of strengthening the bond of affection between our people and ourselves. For it is on such occasions that the heart is tender and susceptible and if they are followed up by the spiritual pastor, with the manifestation of deep personal interest and concern, they will create an atmosphere in which the greatest possibilities of influence and leadership may be realized.

Finally, it ought to be borne in mind that in these happy days of parochial activity, in which there are so many worthy causes and objects likely to appeal to people, one great reward of our pastoral visiting should be to find workers both among the youth and adults of our flock, and to assign each one to some congenial and worthy undertaking. It is only as we can enlist our people in some definite department of Christian endeavor, that we promote their highest spiritual happiness. Work for Christ and the church is the real salvation of our faith. " He that doeth my will," saith our Lord, " shall know of the doctrine," and " He that loseth his life," in love and interest for others, shall find it again in the best and most satisfying experiences of religion.

While no other calling in life places a man under such heavy responsibilities as that of a cure of souls, yet in none is the distribution of one's time so absolutely under one's control. The merchant, the banker, the doctor, the laborer, all other classes of men who respect themselves desire to be reckoned among the workers of the world. For the gospel of work, the average American has a profound respect. The clergyman has this distinction among the various vocations of life. Unlike other workers of the world, he can map out his days and hours to suit himself. It is true that his public ministrations on Sunday are generally a fixed quantity, but his week-days are largely, if not entirely, subject to his own ordering. This is at once a great privilege, and an equally great peril. Woe to the clergyman who says to himself, when his Sunday duties are over, " Thank Heaven I am now free for a whole week." What a temptation to the indolent man to follow the line of least resistance and waste his time and opportunity. Such a type of man in the ministry enables us to understand the layman who said he had four brothers, of whom three worked for their living, while the fourth was a preacher. While the parson is no longer, as that old Saxon word used to connote, always the chief person in the community in dignity and influence, it is safe to assert that his life is more critically if not severely judged than others.

It ought to be evident, not only from the quality of our sermons on Sunday, but from our active interest in our people and the welfare of our community, that we deserve to be classed among the busiest of workers. We have been emancipated by our people from the necessity of working for our daily bread just in order, that with all our gifts of mind and heart, we may freely devote ourselves to the highest interests of

PARISH VISITING

our fellowmen. The life of a clergyman has
in it the possibility of the greatest happiness, for
his compensations are so satisfying. But his
highest rewards can only come to him whose
devotion is so complete that a life of ease and
self-indulgence has ceased to tempt him.

VI

THE PARSON AS A BUSINESS MAN

"Owe no man anything but to love one an-other" is an apostolic injunction much needed by the clergy in these modern days. The failure to heed its advice has proven a fatal pitfall into which many a well meaning parson has been ensnared.

It would be well if a chair of business and commercial ethics could be established and well endowed in all of our theological seminaries. It is possible that the training thereby made available in the practical affairs of everyday life, might save many a man from humiliating embar-rassment and loss of moral power and influence. As it is at present, the average young man called to the ministry passes through the academy, uni-versity, and theological school, and thence to ordi-nation, often blissfully ignorant of the most elementary principles of ordinary business life. He is an "Innocent Abroad" thrust out into a world that is merciless in its verdict upon him if he fails to observe the canons of prompt payment and avoidance of debt. It is entirely right and proper that the community should judge a man whose profession is to teach others how to live, by a standard higher than that applied to the layman. Hence the absolute necessity of setting an example in our dealings with our fellowmen which is entirely above reproach and criticism.

We are quite well aware how easy it is to excuse one's self for such delinquencies on the ground of inadequate salaries. The income of the average clergyman is meager and makes a demand upon him for the exercise of a most careful and well regulated economy. It is said that next to the professors and teachers in colleges and public schools, no class of public servants is more inadequately compensated financially than the ministers of religion.

But with reference to this matter of salary,

several considerations should be borne in mind. In the first place, the clergyman knows in advance that in entering upon the ministry as a vocation, he is supposed to have renounced all hope of worldly gain, and to have set his affections on compensations of an entirely different nature, though by no means less satisfying. We as clergymen therefore are receiving in the way of worldly reward just what we were promised, and therefore ought not to complain. But in the second place, we all know that our highest happiness and greatest influence among men does not depend on what we have, but upon what we are; that character and not money is what makes for spiritual influence and edification. For our comfort and inspiration we have the example of our great Master, who was poorer than poverty itself, and had not where to lay His head; and likewise, we have the example of all his apostles, who, without land or money or any earthly possessions, through faith, subdued kingdoms, wrought righteousness, obtained promises, stopped the mouths of lions.

THE PARSON AS A BUSINESS MAN

We say this, not to justify or defend the small salaries so often paid the clergy, for that practice is often indefensible, but simply that we may lay the emphasis where it rightly belongs, not on the money we receive, but on the service we render to God and our fellowmen. It is entirely true that the people do not appreciate at full value such service. We once heard of an instance which occurred in another communion than our own, in which a good and faithful minister had been promised $600 a year. He was so acceptable to the people, and had done so much to build up the congregation and develop the work, that his trustees met and unanimously voted to increase his salary from six hundred to eight hundred dollars a year. After taking this action, on which they congratulated themselves, they gave their popular minister a large reception to which the whole congregation was invited. At a given signal the chairman of the Board of Trustees arose and announced to the clergyman the good news of the increase. They were a little surprised to see that the information did not seem to give him unmixed pleasure, but that a look of strange sadness came over his face. When the cheering was over, the minister said, " Brethren, I thank you for your kind intentions in my behalf, and for your appreciation of my work; but I cannot possibly accept the additional salary. Indeed I have such hard work now to raise the six hundred which you promised me, but never paid, that if I were to add to this burden another two hundred dollars, I should not even have time to say my prayers."

We believe that the laborer is worthy of his hire, and that where the people can afford it, their clergy should be more generously provided for, not so much because they ask it, but in order that they may thus be relieved of all worldly care and anxiety, and enabled to devote themselves more fully to the discharge of their sacred functions. Moreover, we are glad to recognize the fact that in this respect there has been a decided improvement in recent years.

But whatever may be the changes in store for the future, it is not at all probable that the time will ever come when the ministry can be regarded as a lucrative profession, or as one that does not call upon those who exercise it to practice economy, simplicity, and self-denial. Indeed, it would be a grievous calamity to our sacred calling, if it did not appeal to our heroism and faith and find us ready to endure any hardship for the privilege of proclaiming the unsearchable riches of Christ. The man who enters the ministry, because he regards it an easy profession, has doomed himself to a well deserved and ignominious failure on the very threshold of his undertaking.

Our chief concern at present in what we are about to say is, that taking the situation as we find it, we should adjust ourselves to it, and strive to acquit ourselves in all our financial and fiduciary relations as men of honor and stainless probity.

To this end we should realize that nothing so destroys the helpful influence of a clergyman, and injures his fair name in the community, as the reputation of being careless and slovenly

about money matters. As soon as the young
clergyman is settled in his first parish, the
butcher, the baker, and the business community
generally, begin to take his measure as to promptness in meeting his obligations. The trades-
people are usually very kind and accommodating.
All they ask is that a man shall conscientiously
keep his word with them, and assure them by
his conduct to the very last degree, that he is
possessed of the strictest sense of personal honor.
This will require at times some effort on his part,
for his salary may not be promptly paid, small
as it is, and the necessities of his household may
be pressing upon him. But by adhering loyally
and firmly to his principle, and paying promptly
those to whom he is indebted, he will soon bring
a moral pressure to bear upon his congregation
to treat him honorably in turn. Vestries all
know that everybody is ready to trust a clergyman, for they are aware that his life depends on
his good name, and for this very reason, they
are often careless about their financial obligations to him until he seems almost compelled to

go into debt to meet his expenses. Before he realizes the harm that has come to him the evil is done.

Let him therefore have a clear understanding with his Vestry at the very beginning, and hold them firmly to it, that his salary shall be paid without failure, on a certain day of each month. Then let him regulate his expenses accordingly, making it a rule to lay by in store each pay day, a small balance for emergencies. Let him live within his income, be it large or small. Such insistence on his part with his vestry for a clear understanding, will help them and the whole parish to treat their obligations to him in a fair and honorable Christian manner.

It is an outrage at once against good manners and good morals, that while the ordinary layman will promptly pay every other bill and obligation he owes, he frequently discharges his church obligations only when it suits his convenience or not at all. The clergyman who pursues a business-like course such as I have described, will therefore be conferring a real blessing upon the parish and community he serves by assuming from the very start that his people are going to be honest and straight-forward in meeting all their church and parochial dues. We speak not only from personal experience, but from intimate knowledge of the lives of hundreds of clergymen, and from an observation extending over many years when we say that it is impossible to exaggerate the importance of regularly meeting all liabilities and keeping square with the world.

Moreover, if it is so vital to a clergyman's influence that he should be so careful about his own financial affairs, it is equally so when he is dealing with money not his own. There are certain funds, such as the communion alms, gifts for charitable objects, missionary collections and others of a special nature, which are likely from time to time to pass through his hands in the absence of the proper treasurer. Again donations may be intrusted to a clergyman for certain specified objects. In all such cases, great care should be taken to pass the money on without delay to its proper custodian or destination, and a receipt taken to show that this has been done. Offerings are frequently received at services when the parish treasurer is not present. In such instances if possible let two men of the congregation count it in the vestry room, and transmit it to the treasurer, enclosing a voucher over their own signature. It is a wise provision that obtains in many parishes, that two men shall always serve as accountants after each service where an offering is received. Such a practice begets confidence, and is a protection to the treasurer as well as to the clergyman. But it ought to be the invariable rule of the rector never to handle any of the funds of the parish when it is possible to avoid it.

The demand for publicity which one hears constantly at the present day in connection with the financial affairs of all commercial enterprises should not be disregarded by the church.

While the rector of a parish is supposed to concern himself about its spiritualities, rather than its temporalities, he certainly has the right to insist that his parish treasurer render an accurate account at the vestry meetings of all expenses together with the balance sheet; and it would be helpful if the congregation could be systematically informed of the financial condition of the church from time to time.

There are few, if any, parishes so ideally administered that the rector can afford to repudiate all responsibility for the management of its financial affairs. It must frequently happen that his counsel is most valuable, and he can always exert his influence towards securing a wise, efficient, and progressive policy. The financial affairs of a parish will not run of themselves, and the vestry must feel that they have behind them the deep interest, intelligent sympathy, and sane judgment of their pastor. His influence is often valuable in suggesting the names of men of high Christian integrity and devotion to serve on the vestry, and if the administration of the business affairs of his church commends itself to the community, his spiritual influence will be the greater and he will be the more highly esteemed.

In bringing this chapter to a close, we should

like to suggest to the clergy that perhaps the most important officer in the vestry is the parish treasurer. There are many lamentable instances where this office is filled by men who consider their duty is fully discharged when they receive the money placed in their hands, and render an account of it. It does not occur to them that it is their great privilege, as well as their bounden duty, to develop, enlarge, and improve the giving power and disposition of the congregation; to see that all subscriptions are promptly gathered in, and to watch their opportunity to secure new subscribers, and from time to time, to do what they can to induce those who already give to increase their offerings if they find it possible. The chief financial difficulty that exists in our various parishes may frequently be laid at the door of vestrymen who utterly fail to give the church the benefit of their best business energy and skill, and above all of parish treasurers who could not hold such a position in any other corporation through sheer inefficiency and neglect of duty.

VII

THE PARSON AS A CITIZEN

A clergyman is not only a priest of God and an ambassador for Christ, but he is also a citizen of the community in which he lives, and of the country under the protection of whose flag he enjoys certain inestimable privileges. The apostle says, "Let every soul be subject unto the higher powers, for there is no power but of God; the powers that be are ordained of God. Render therefore to all their dues; tribute to whom tribute is due, custom to whom custom; fear to whom fear; honor to whom honor."

There is a natural temptation to confine one's interest and influence and service entirely to one's own flock, but a minister should recognize his wider relations to the welfare of his city, and to the nation in which he lives. He should be on the side of law and order and good government. Those placed in authority to enforce the observance of decency and good morals should always be able to find in him, a friend ready to give the weight of his position to the promotion of civil betterment.

We are living in an age when social service, or the application of the life and teaching of Christ to the various conditions of humanity, is being emphasized as never before. This spirit of Christian altruism urges us to concern ourselves, not only in what men believe, but in the kind of lives they lead, and how they are clothed and fed and sheltered. In all this we should rejoice because, among other reasons, it so largely broadens and increases our sphere of usefulness. This quickened sense of personal responsibility for the social and economic welfare of our fellowmen lays upon the minister of to-day a correspondingly greater opportunity.

There was a time in the history of the church's life when a public service on Sunday, with perhaps a sermon, morning and evening, constituted a very large share of his work and responsibility.

87

To-day all this is changed. Frequently there is a daily service, and the parish church is the center of an activity which finds expression in many organizations, having for their object the advancement of the Kingdom along many lines. The church cannot afford to be indifferent to anything that concerns the physical, moral, mental, or spiritual life of a man. For instance, it is not foreign to a minister's duty for him to inquire as to the purity of the water which the people drink, and whence its supply. If it is not satisfactory, to ascertain what is being done by the community, or its representatives in the city council to safeguard it against contamination and to see that an abundant supply of this necessity of life is furnished to all the people. How about the sewerage upon which the health of the entire community must depend? Is it no concern of the minister of Christ that the people should be protected against·malaria and typhoid germs, and the very best sanitation possible secured to that end? You probably have a county poor house in your neighborhood. Have you ever visited it, and do you find the atmosphere there as wholesome, and the condition of the inmates as comfortable as it could be made? Are these unfortunate people treated with kindness and Christian consideration? Do they enjoy the privilege of having regular services supplied by yourself and others? What plan has been adopted for the relief of the poor not thus provided for? Have you formed a charitable association, perhaps in connection with other ministers, with an intelligent and humane secretary at its head, to whom applicants for relief may be sent, with the assurance that each case will be carefully investigated, and worthy appeals promptly met?

What steps have you taken towards regulating, if not abolishing the saloon evil in your community, whereby so many young men are tempted to their destruction, and so many homes are wrecked? What place in your community has been provided where a young man can drop in of an evening and meet congenial friends, and have an innocent game of cards or pool, instead of frequenting a saloon? Have you a Y. M. C. A.

89

within reach, and if so, what is your personal
and official relation towards it? Are you aware
that this organization was founded by, and is a
product of our church, and that your influence
can do much to prevent it from degenerating
into another religious sect? In short, what are
you doing to provide and encourage the right kind
of amusement and recreation among the young
people and others? Have you organized a company of boy scouts? Have you a play-ground
association, providing places where the boys and
girls out of school hours can secure ample opportunity for physical exercise and fresh air? Are
the streets of your town kept clean and in good
order, and free from indecent and sensational
advertising of all kinds? In what condition are
the roads and public highways, and can anything
be done to arouse the community to bring about
their improvement?

There are many occasions when it may be wise
to coöperate with the ministers of the other religious bodies and their congregations in further-
ing needed reforms and improvements. Such as

the establishment and maintenance of a good public library; the promotion of the best interests of the public schools which as a citizen you should visit regularly, taking care that competent teachers are employed and retained, and that the buildings are well equipped and well ventilated and sanitary.

In these days of the prevalence of the White Plague, there will be frequent opportunities for the clergy to show their interest in suffering humanity by coöperating and establishing sanitaria where those afflicted can enjoy the best chance of recovery. If there is a hospital in your community, the clergyman will naturally take a deep interest in its welfare, and besides visiting the patients where he can be of service, will do all he can to promote its efficiency.

I mention these various instances as furnishing abundant scope for the minister to show himself a good citizen, public spirited, broad minded, and genuinely alive to everything that appertains to the physical, intellectual, moral, as well as spiritual well-being of his city.

A BISHOP'S MESSAGE

Of course it would be easy to object that a clergyman is not ordained for such duties and should confine himself exclusively to his spiritual ministrations and leave to others, whose special business it is, to attend to these quasi-secular interests. But such reasoning is not only narrow and unphilosophical, but ignores the obvious truth that whatever promotes the true well-being and uplift of a community has an intimate relation to the Christian welfare of the people.

It ought not to be necessary for us to say that we are not advocating that the clergy should leave the "word of God" and "serve tables," but that we are simply pleading for the cultivation of a spirit of keen and unselfish interest which leads one to regard the sacred office as a trust committed to him for the benefit of the whole community in all that concerns it.

The same broad-minded spirit should characterize the clergyman's relations with the ministers of the various religious bodies into which the average American town is almost sure to be divided. Regarded from a purely diplomatic and common sense point of view, it ought to be evident to any thoughtful man that the esteem, good will, and friendship, of those who are appointed by their people as leaders of the religious life of a place, are valuable assets to his influence for good.

There need not be the slightest compromise of our faith or doctrinal position by encouraging such an attitude of mutual regard, while at the same time it will enable us to work together on many lines of common interest, involving no ecclesiastical question whatever.

It need hardly be said in this connection that cherishing such a kindly and truly Christian spirit of courtesy and forebearance, does not even suggest the official recognition of the various theological views and opinions which cause men to differ. At the same time it does mean, that by maintaining such an attitude towards all who love our Lord in sincerity, we are helping to create an atmosphere in which any contribution we may have to make towards bringing about a better understanding will have some hope of being entertained.

This spirit of broad-minded citizenship in the body of Christ is all the more incumbent upon the clergy at the present time when our own church has formally committed herself to the great enterprise of trying to bring about Christian Unity.

It was with this idea in view that the last Lambeth Conference laid such emphasis on the importance, on our part, of seeking every opportunity to coöperate with those of our Christian Brethren, chiefly in order, that by a free fraternal interchange of opinion we could at once ascertain their views and have the privilege, under the most favorable conditions, of imparting our own.

VIII

VARIOUS TYPES OF CHURCHMAN-
SHIP

The preface to our American book of Common Prayer opens with this rather suggestive and remarkable statement: " It is a most invaluable part of that blessed liberty wherewith Christ hath made us free, that in His worship, different forms and usages may without offense be allowed, provided the substance of the faith be kept entire; and that, in every church, what cannot be clearly determined to belong to Doctrine, may be referred to Discipline; and therefore by common consent and authority, may be altered, abridged, enlarged, amended, or otherwise disposed of, as may seem most convenient for the edification of the people, according to the various exigencies of times and occasions."

Herein certain principles are laid down.

A BISHOP'S MESSAGE

First, that in the worship of the church there is a certain blessed liberty guaranteed us. Secondly, that in the exercise of this liberty in worship, different forms and usages may, without offense, be allowed, provided the substance of the faith be kept entire. And thirdly, that these may be altered, abridged, enlarged, amended, or otherwise disposed of, by common consent and authority as may seem most convenient for the edification of the people.

In the exercise of this liberty thus guaranteed and regulated by law there has grown up in the public worship of the church more or less variety in the rendering of the services according to differing tastes of individual ministers and their congregations.

While in every congregation, in every Diocese throughout the church, the same form of service as prescribed by the prayer book is supposed to be used, large freedom is permitted in the manner of rendering that service. This freedom is generally guaranteed to the clergy in the direction embodied in the rubrics preceding the several parts and offices of the prayer book. The language of some of the rubrics is mandatory, making use of the word " shall "; in others it is discretionary, where the word " may " is employed. In other instances, even where a rubric is mandatory, there is given some discretion as to the manner in which it shall be carried out, as in those cases where it is ordered that a chant " may be said or sung."

It can be readily understood that even in the exercise of this liberty there will naturally grow up a greater or less variety in the rendering of the church's worship. In one congregation everything permissible will be sung, not only the chants but even the prayers and "Amens," including the creeds. While in another, where less music is desired, or possibly where the choir is not so efficient, the music will be limited to that which is absolutely necessary.

A similar variety in the form of rendering the service has grown up in connection with the celebration of the holy communion. The postures of the officiating clergyman and the vestments which on that occasion he may use, as well as the employment of more or less music, are all left largely to the discretion of the minister and congregation, subject, when questions arise, to the authority of the Bishop. With regard to the matter of vestments, there is no law binding upon us, save the law of custom, and even that differs in minor details in various congregations. Great charity should be exercised therefore in condemning a usage simply because we are not accustomed to it. It may be entirely lawful and defensible.

The difference in the matter of rendering the same prayer book service is sometimes so marked by the use of more or less ceremony or music and other adjuncts, all entirely lawful, that one accustomed to worship in a congregation where everything is conducted with the utmost simplicity with little ritual and only the hymns sung, may not find himself entirely at home in a more ornate service.

The story has been told of a low churchman who was the guest in the same city successively of a Roman Catholic and a ritualistic friend. After attending the elaborate service in the latter's church where lights, incense and much ceremony were used, he accompanied his Roman friend to his church. Some one asked him afterwards what his impressions were. He replied that while the former was very beautiful he rather preferred the more simple service of the church of Rome.

It is natural that those who prefer more ceremony should desire to see such use generally prevail, and no less is it to be expected that those to whom a more plain and simple service is acceptable should urge its adoption. Indeed, there was a time, within the memory of the writer, when the difference between a high churchman and a low churchman was chiefly a difference of more or less ritual in the conduct of the service. Moreover, as this love of ritual frequently expressed itself in the celebration of the holy communion, the high churchman or ritualist was supposed to be one who laid special emphasis on that blessed sacrament. He was frequently described as a sacramentarian. Happily for the peace of the church, one hears very little nowadays about high church and low church. The rather intense, and at one time bitter spirit of controversy, has at least compelled men to investigate more deeply the great historic facts on which the church is founded, and to appreciate more than ever that large liberty which may be enjoyed in our communion. Provided the substance of the faith be kept entire, men are quite willing to accord to each other the indulgence of that individual taste which has been so wisely safeguarded by the prayer book. It is greatly to be desired that as members of a church, truly and historically Catholic, we should all not only tolerate, but gladly welcome a wide diversity in things non-essential. The church should be able to adapt herself to all sorts and conditions of men.

Various races of men, with their national characteristics and predilections, are constantly coming into our communion and fellowship, and no one should wish to deny to others the liberty he enjoys himself, or to narrow the true comprehensiveness of the church's worship. A number of instances have occurred where whole congregations of Italians and Slavs have come into our communion with their ministers. It would be folly on the part of the church to deny to them the observance of many customs and ceremonies which have become dear to them, simply because they have not been practiced uniformly by our Anglo-Saxon worshipers.

We are to be congratulated that party feeling among us has so largely disappeared. It is not only inevitable, but entirely fitting, that men should have strong convictions. But the evil arises when we allow such convictions to lead us to withhold our confidence and brotherly esteem, from those who have equally strong convictions, but do not happen to entertain the same view as ourselves. Because we are so sure that we are correct in our opinions, it by no means follows that the brother who differs from us is wrong, or has not the same liberty within the church's law to cherish and defend his position. Narrowness and bigotry are the characteristics of a petty sect and have no place in a great church that has for its inspiring mission the gathering into its broad fold those who come from all the ends of the earth. We would counsel young men entering the ministry not to identify themselves with any school or party, and not to allow themselves to be labeled by any invidious title or shibboleth. Such an attitude on our part does not make for peace, and is likely to hamper our influence and circumscribe our appeal, and render our approach to those whom we seek to reach more difficult.

At the same time, let us try to see the good in all schools of thought, and in all party alignments, for they all represent some aspect of truth; and let us recognize and honor the right of our brother to hold his view and accord to it the hospitality to which it is entitled.

No one can deny the debt of obligation which the church owes to the so-called catholic party, in helping us safeguard the claims of the historic ministry, and the rich sacramental life of the church. Nor yet can one fail to recognize how the low church party has stood loyally for a type of evangelical piety and devotion beyond all praise; while the broad church school has given us a wider view of our relations to the world of thought, and furnished us scholars whose learning would be an ornament to any church.

This spirit of broad and sympathetic comprehensiveness was very characteristic of the late Archbishop Temple when Bishop of London. Indefatigable as a worker himself, he had a great love and reverence for those of his clergy who worked and did things, and got hold of men and built them up in the faith of God. Personally he cared little for ritual, and was a man of severe simplicity of tastes in matters of worship. Rugged and rather brusque as he was in manner, he had the wisdom to recognize the rights of the clergy under his jurisdiction, and always respected them. It is said that on one occasion at a visitation when his Lordship was expected to administer the holy eucharist, a very ritualistic vicar said to him, " Excuse me, my Lord, but we always celebrate in this church standing in front of the altar." " Do you? " was his reply; " well,

I don't," and he proceeded to follow his own practice and stood at the north end. On another occasion when a devoted priest who had served with great self-denial and success a large parish among the poor in London died, it became the duty of Bishop Temple to make an appointment to the vacant living. The late vicar was a very extreme high churchman, and there were many applicants for the place. When at last his Lordship made the appointment, one disappointed candidate who confidently expected to get it, came to Fulham Palace to complain, and to find out why he had not been chosen. He said he belonged to the same school of churchmanship as the late vicar, and was his dear personal friend; that in his own church, he observed every point of ritual, and followed every ceremony that had been practiced in the vacant parish which he sought. "No, you don't," said the Bishop. "I beg your pardon, my Lord," said the candidate, "but I am sure I do. Can you mention any difference?" "Yes, I can," replied the Bishop. "Have you a Bambino in your church?" "A

Bambino, my Lord? No, I have not." "Ah, there it is," said the Lord Bishop; "those people are used to a Bambino, and I appointed a man to serve them who had one." All schools and parties could feel that Bishop Temple was entirely fair, and that there was only one condition or qualification on which he insisted, and that was that a man should be godly and devoted to the saving of souls.

When one has passed many years in the full activity of the church's life and progress, he learns among other things, to lay emphasis on things that are fundamentally important, and to place first things first.

IX

THE PARSON AMONG HIS BOOKS

One can generally form a fairly correct idea of the intellectual life and habits of a clergyman by spending a few minutes in his study. No matter how small his salary, if he be a man keenly alive to the responsibility of his high calling, he will manage somehow to gather about him at least a few of the indispensable working books of his great profession. He will not only have the Bible, and at least some of the best and most recent commentators upon the various books, but his insatiable intellectual craving and bias will betray themselves by having at hand his volume of Shakespeare, his Browning, Dante, Tennyson, his Macaulay, and Gibbon, " Green's History of the English," Emerson's Essays and other standard books. There will also be on his table the *Living Church,* the *Churchman,* the *Southern*

Churchman, the *Outlook,* and perhaps the *Literary Digest.* One or two of the best monthly magazines, such as *Harper's* or *Scribner's,* or the *Atlantic Monthly* will also be in evidence.

No clergyman can plead poverty nowadays as an excuse for not having a fairly well equipped if small library. Nearly every diocese has a lending library where all the best new books can be secured. Besides this, there is in every diocese, a branch of the Church Periodical Club, which has for its express object the supplying to clergymen new books, magazines, and all necessary literature. Still further to sweep away every excuse in nearly every town one generally finds a free public library.

With such facilities at his command, we must conclude that a clergyman who has not provided himself with good books is either ignorant as to the source of supply, or even sadder still, that he does not care for literature, is not a reading man, and therefore is starving his own intellectual and spiritual life and doling out to his people Sunday after Sunday only such meager and innutritious food as he may be able to evolve from the depths of his inner consciousness. Such a man ought not to be surprised, if the hungry sheep, whom he has been appointed to feed, and to lead in the fresh and green pastures, have ceased to look any longer to him for nourishment, and have gradually strayed into other folds. Woe be to the Spiritual leader of the flock if he has failed to replenish his store house of well garnered material by constantly adding to it what he has gained from converse with other minds.

Intellectual stagnation is nearly always the precursor of spiritual decay and death. If, on Sunday, the people do not flock to God's house to hear our message, would it not be at least a counsel of prudence for us to ask ourselves whether after all we have a message worth their hearing. Is it or is it not true that everywhere the man whose soul is afire with a message from God is sure to have those in increasing numbers who are eager to receive it? But such a message as will inspire and help others must first have found a lodgment in our own hearts. It can only come to us by prayer, meditation and study.

When once the truth we desire to present has taken possession of us, we must seek by every means within our power to illustrate it and bring it home to the hearts of our people. It is only out of the abundance of a well-filled mind that this can be done. The mind must be fed and stimulated by appropriating and making our own the thoughts and inspiration of others. Some one has said, " Beware of the man of one book." This aphorism may be interpreted as a warning against a too discursive habit of reading, and as a commendation of the importance of thoroughly mastering a few good books. There is certainly enough truth in it to suggest to us that there is one book with which we cannot be too familiar. The study of God's word, with the vast mass of literature which has been produced to illustrate and enforce it, is in itself a most worthy employ-ment of one's life.

But it is not to disparage the importance of the Bible that we urge upon the clergyman to culti-vate an intimacy with other books as well.   Indeed, all truth is related, and we shall find in every great book that has made its deep impress upon the minds of thoughtful men, ideas which throw light upon the Bible. Every great poet or dramatist or novelist, whose genius has interpreted to us human life, and revealed the motives that govern and control the human heart, has contributed to the illumination of the Bible.

But let us first consider the study of the Bible. There is no doubt that among the people generally, it is a sadly neglected book. One often finds an elegant copy of it with gilt clasps, resting as an ornament upon the table perhaps in the drawing room, but it is pathetic to contemplate how seldom it is opened; and with the neglect of Bible reading at home, there has come a widespread disregard of family prayer, the saying of grace at meals, and the observance of any reverent form or ceremony calculated to impress the children of the household with the conviction that their parents esteem religion as fundamental in the family life. This popular ignorance of the

Bible makes it all the more necessary that the clergyman should not only be familiar with its text and meaning, but that his preaching should be saturated through and through with its spirit and should derive its reënforcement and power and high sanctions from its sacred pages. The only way by which a man can get religion, says Thomas Carlyle, is to receive it from some soul who has it. It is not only the dry, intellectual assent to certain dogmatic truths, but it is a life of love and loyalty and devotion, inspired by the personal Christ to whom we have given our hearts.

Herein is the unique power and excellence of the Holy Bible. It is a perfect store-house of religious experience, written by men whose lives have sounded the depth and length and height and breadth of the surpassing love of God. We clergymen who teach the Christian religion must catch the spirit of those men. Otherwise, the true glory of the Bible will be a hidden glory to us. Merely as literature, the Bible stands alone in the world of letters.   But its chief value is that it reveals to men the love of God as manifested in human lives.

We have sometimes been amazed at the ignorance of men seeking ordination, as to the contents of the Bible.   It is incumbent upon us to master this book.   If we can read it in the original language in which it was given to us, all the better.   Happily now, a fair knowledge of the Greek Testament is supposed to be a necessary prerequisite to ordination.   But the King James Version is a marvelous repository of English undefiled.   To be able to quote it, and to quote it accurately and freely, in illustration of our truth, is a most desirable achievement.   We have noticed that English preachers make far more extensive use of the Bible than we Americans are wont to do.   They probably know it better.   We should study it by books as well as by subjects.   We should study it biographically as well as theologically.   Above all should our new Testament be so absolutely at our tongue's end, that we can draw upon it with readiness and power, to drive home our appeal. There never was a time when more interest was taken by scholars in the Bible, or when more good books have been written to explain and interpret it. Therefore to be ignorant of this great source of our authority and power is the more inexcusable.

But there are many other books of which the well equipped clergyman cannot afford to be ignorant. There is a vast world of idealism and high inspiration awaiting the intimate acquaintance with your Shakespeare and Dante and Schiller and Tennyson; your Milton and Cowper and Wordsworth; your Lowell and Longfellow, and many another poet in the long list that might be named. If you do not care for poetry cultivate a love for it. Be assured the fault is not with the poets. You are on trial, not they.

Then the clergyman will learn to delight in history. He will regard it as a revelation of God's dealing with the human race, and it will be full of suggestive illustrations in his preaching. The philosophy of history will reassure our faith, and convince us of the providential ordering of God in the affairs of men.

The Pastor of souls will not fail, moreover, to enrich his fancy and broaden his outlook upon the world by reading at least a few of the standard works of fiction both old and new. Sir Walter Scott, Charles Dickens, Thackeray, George Eliot, among the older English masters, and many a modern work of fiction may well arrest his attention.

Indeed the whole realm of literature, art, science and philosophy will invite and fascinate us if we abandon ourselves to its charm. The great difficulty will be to make a wise discrimination.

In all we have said, we have not forgotten the limitation of time and opportunity which confront the busy minister; but we also know beyond a shadow of a doubt, that the chief difficulty is not to be ascribed to a lack of time, but too often to a lack of interest, and an absence of that passion for knowledge and self-improvement so vital to all progress. We do not mean a pride of learning for its own sake, but that nobler impulse which leads a man, called to do the greatest work for God and humanity, to prepare himself in a manner commensurate with the dignity of his calling, that he may do it superbly well.

We remember with the keenest pleasure two or three days spent at Farnham Palace, as the guest of Dr. Thorold, then the Lord Bishop of Winchester. We observed among his books what seemed to be a complete edition of the sermons of Spurgeon, Liddon, and Phillips Brooks. Taking down from their shelves some of these books we observed that they had been read and marked and underlined, and showed every indication of having been thoroughly studied. We asked the Lord Bishop to which of these three great preachers he felt most indebted. He paused for a moment and then replied that at one time he would have said Spurgeon; that Canon Liddon had also been very suggestive; but of recent years our own Phillips Brooks had seemed to appeal to him more strongly, and that he rarely left home without slipping a volume of Brooks in his bag. The young man trying to learn how to preach will not ignore these great masters, but he will study them rather to catch their spirit, perhaps their style and method of treatment than for any servile imitation. There is much homiletic literature published to-day, which, if used with discrimination, will be most helpful. But nothing can take the place of hard study.

In all we endeavor to set forth on this subject, our aim has been to encourage and stimulate the clergyman to address himself with enthusiasm to the delightful task of self-culture through good literature and study. It is sad to contemplate how men deprive themselves so often of the companionship and inspiration of the greatest and best thoughts that have enriched the world and remain content to live in an atmosphere of the commonplace, when they might enjoy converse with the noblest spirits. A man is utterly without excuse who deliberately condemns himself to such monotony of existence, and is committing a crime at once against himself, his people, and his sacred calling.

In order to pursue a course of reading and persist in it courageously, our time must be jealously safeguarded and it must be understood that our mornings are sacredly set apart for this great and most necessary undertaking. We shall not forfeit the respect and confidence of our people by adhering tenaciously to such a rule, but on the contrary, they will honor us the more for our evident determination to improve ourselves in order to give them the fruit of our best intellectual and spiritual achievement. We are thus paying our people the highest compliment and at the same time adopting the only plan whereby we can serve them worthily.

X

MAKING USE OF THE LAITY

The title of this chapter is perhaps not altogether felicitous, but we hope to make our meaning sufficiently clear as we proceed. It is at once most vital to our own success and to the spiritual development of our people that we know how to interest the individual member of our flock in some definite line of Christian work.

It was a favorite and characteristic principle of one of the most efficient pastors whom we have ever known to do nothing himself which he could possibly persuade some one else to do equally well. We once knew a clergyman sent to take charge of a certain mission whose governing principles were just the opposite; namely, never to ask any one to do anything which he could possibly do himself. He rang the bell of the little church, made the fires, and even swept the floor.

MAKING USE OF THE LAITY

Being especially anxious to impress his Bishop
with the idea that he was a tremendous and indefatigable worker, he took occasion to carry
through the street from the neighboring Rectory
an armful of wood for the church stove just as
his Bishop, accompanied by his chaplain, arrived.
It would have been amusing had it not been so
pathetic to see the dear old parson puffing away
under his heavy load, sure of his Bishop's warm
commendation.

Of course it was very easy for this good
brother to say that no one else had offered to do
this menial service. At the same time, another
clergyman, possessing the gift of interesting people, would have found a number of good women
who would have considered it a privilege to take
turns in keeping the church in order and men and
boys to tend the fire and ring the bell and relieve
their clergyman of such work. How could any
Bishop fail to see that this clergyman, by this very
act, so far from showing himself a great worker,
proved that he was a pitiable failure, in that he
did not have the ability to call to his aid and en-

list the coöperation of others who would have been glad to help him?

In every parish or mission, however small, there are those who love to be of real service, if only the opportunity is given them and the responsibility placed upon them. If people can only be made to feel that they are really needed, and that their help will be appreciated, it is seldom that they will not take pleasure in coöperating with the rector.

It is for the minister to find out the various gifts and aptitudes of his people, and then assign to each one that work for which he is best fitted. Of course there are difficulties to be overcome. In some instances he will be disappointed by persons refusing to enlist, no matter how great the need, but as a rule he will be surprised to find with what readiness helpers will come to his rescue, when once the invitation is extended, and the personal appeal is made to render a real service in some good cause.

At the present time when so much interest is being taken in questions relating to social service

in its various ramifications, there is an unprece-
dented call for Christian workers and hence an
unusual opportunity for the employment of various kinds of talent. We once knew a very respectable layman who took but little interest in the
church work, and rarely attended the services,
to become quite an enthusiastic worker by being
appointed to a position as choir monitor. He
knew little about music, but his rector had ascer-
tained that he had a sort of genius for managing
young men and boys, and that they liked him.
He became responsible for their presence in the
choir at the Sunday services, for their reverent behavior, promptness, neatness and order about
their vestments, and was a sort of master of ceremonies at the Processionals. That particular office was created for him, and in discharging its
duties, he almost unconsciously became interested
in the other activities of the parish.

One of the most anxious problems that confronts the clergyman in small parishes is to secure teachers for the Sunday school. Men and
women hesitate to engage in such work frequently

because they honestly feel themselves so poorly equipped in technical religious knowledge as to be unfit for it. This reluctance may often be overcome by the tactful pastor, if he will form a class, taught by himself, of those who are willing to be prepared for this particular work. Such a class might meet either on Sunday, as a sort of normal Bible class, or on some convenient evening in the week. It ought to be borne in mind by the minister that every one thus induced to engage in such personal service, is not only helping others, but is being enormously helped himself by the very efforts required to bless and enrich other lives.

Work among young men and boys, through such organizations as the boy scouts, St. Andrew Brotherhoods, boys' missionary societies and clubs, affords an opportunity to interest many men whose Christian lives at present are not developed by means of any definite work in behalf of others. Among young women and girls there are such societies as the Girl's Friendly, the Daughters of the King, the Woman's Auxiliary, the Junior Auxiliary, various kinds of guilds for the reverent care of the chancel and altar and vestments which supply the occasion for enrolling many others among the list of active helpers in the parish.

It is almost a self-evident truth that unless every Christian man and woman is engaged in some particular kind of impersonal service, their own spiritual life will wither and decay. It is not only, therefore, for the sake of the work always waiting to be done, but quite as much for the rich blessing vouchsafed to the workers themselves that the wise rector is so anxious to bring out the latent energies of people which otherwise would lie dormant.

It has often been remarked, and we fear with much truth, that our beloved church especially fails in laying under tribute the active help of the laity. Among our Christian Brethren of the Methodists, Presbyterians, Baptists and other communions, it seems to be taken for granted that all church members will become workers in the various organizations, and we find them in large numbers enrolled as Sunday school and Bible teachers, as well as in the various missionary societies. Unhappily in our own church this is frequently not the case.

It is said that in the days of the great prosperity of St. George's parish, New York, which was famous as a working parish, a large family applied to the rector to be received as members. He asked them what kind of work they desired to engage in severally. Was it missionary work, Sunday school work, social service work, visiting among the tenements, or what? Which especially appealed to them? They looked a little embarrassed and hesitated. At last the head of the family replied, " Oh, we wish to come to St. George's because we like to hear you preach, but we do not wish to do any church work." " Well, now, my good friends," said the rector, " let me tell you that I think you have come to the wrong place. If you do not propose to work, you had better go to the church on Fifth Avenue, known as the Church of the Heavenly Rest; here everybody works." Perhaps we ought to say that despite its name so suggestive of ease, the Fifth Avenue church is also characterized by a spirit of earnest Christian activity.

It is too often the case with us that the typical Episcopalian may be described as the prosperous business man who goes to church only on Sunday morning, pays his pew rent, helps to make up the yearly deficit reported at the Easter vestry meeting, and complacently allows the rector to carry on the spiritual work of the parish as he best may. Just so far as this is a fair description of the average vestryman among us, it is in vain to hope that the church will accomplish in any community the great spiritual work for which it was established. Such purely formal and conventional Christianity as we have pictured is too often, we are persuaded, the fault of the rector himself. This very vestryman probably was prepared for confirmation by this clergyman. At that susceptible moment in his life, when, if ever, his heart was tender, and his emotions awakened, he should have been made to realize that the Christian calling meant personal service for

Christ, and that the church expected him to lend his influence and example to the maintenance of high ideals of loyalty and devotion. He should have been put to work at once.

No plea of professional or business pre-occupation can justify the utter repudiation of the law of active service. Indeed, it is generally found that the larger a man's business is, and the heavier his responsibilities in the commercial world, the greater is his opportunity for service, and the more telling is his example. The men who can do things in the business world and stand for power and efficiency, are the very men who are most needed to do the work of God. It is a strong man's work, preëminently worthy of our highest and best gifts of heart and brain. No one can overestimate the added strength and vigor and dignity which would come into the life of our parishes, if the men who stand for social and commercial leadership in all our communities, would not only give their money, but themselves to the service of God and could be led to identify themselves with the church's spiritual mission and with a courageous and manly devotion, take a man's part in forwarding its great work.

There is another vocation for the earnest layman, of which the clergyman should avail himself far more generally than is now the practice among us. We refer to the use of lay-readers and lay-preachers. It is the unique privilege and great advantage of our church to have a form of public worship at once simple, dignified and impressive, which can be rendered by the layman with much edification. In visiting many of the country parishes in England, one is impressed by finding that the Lessons at morning and evening prayer are generally read by the Squire or Warden, or some other honored layman who stands high in the community. It was the invariable custom for Mr. Gladstone, Prime Minister of England, to read the Lessons at St. Stephen's, Hawarden, where his son was the rector. This practice is one that might well be more frequently adopted in our American church. The reading of the lessons by the Wardens and other members of the Vestry, and persons appointed for this function by the rector, and duly licensed by the Bishop, might become a means of training in every parish a small body of competent and intelligent lay-readers, who could not only officiate in the absence of the rector, but might be licensed by the Bishop to make addresses whenever there was occasion, and it could be done with edification. Where the reading is well performed, as it frequently is, it is not only acceptable to the congregation, but it tends to develop in the person who thus officiates a more intelligent and sympathetic interest in the services and the church generally, and on that account amply justifies the practice.

But it is not only in the local parish church that lay-readers may frequently be used to great advantage. Within easy reach of all our churches, whether in city or country districts, there are villages, hamlets, school houses, and rural communities, where our services are unknown, and often such places are without any religious services whatsoever. Such localities open up a large field for missionary work which can be conducted by devoted men. The more widely these laymen are known and honored in the several communities where they happen to live, the more such effort on their part to carry the beautiful services of our church to those in reach of them, will be appreciated, and the more good will result from such voluntary help.

While much is still to be desired in the matter of utilizing in various ways the assistance of the laity in church work, it is a source of reëncouragement and hope for the future to note how much progress has been made in this direction in recent years. In a number of Dioceses, lay-readers' associations have been formed, and conventions are regularly held where interesting reports are made of work accomplished in establishing new mission stations, centers of church work, and the founding of new parishes. In some of our cities, missionary guilds of lay-readers have accomplished the building up of Sunday schools in strategic localities which give promise of growing into self-supporting parishes in the near future. Other guilds of laymen maintain services each Sunday in adjoining towns and villages which are under the general supervision of a clergyman whose chief duty is to follow up the work and minister to the stations thus called into existence by the enterprise and zeal of earnest laymen. Still more noteworthy has been the Laymen's Missionary Movement, inaugurated a few years ago by earnest men in the various religious bodies, among whom our own laymen have been prominent to a degree altogether gratifying.

Let the clergyman realize that the only true test of the permanence and spiritual value of his work is not the number of names entered upon his parish register as belonging to his church, but the personal interest taken by those who have named the name of Christ as evinced by lives of active Christian service. Every one thus aroused to enlist on the honor roll of workers for Christ will not only bless others, but will himself be richly blessed.

XI

THE PARSON AS A MAN
AMONG MEN

"This one thing I do," was the working program of a famous Christian missionary and a most inspiring example in the art of winning men for God. This phrase might be interpreted in the terms of modern life as meaning that a clergyman should never lose sight of the supreme dignity and importance of the great work to which God has called him into the ministry of reconciliation, and to which he has consecrated his life. If, in the midst of all the activities of his busy calling, his one deep abiding purpose is to serve his fellow-men and by word and good example lead them to embrace and ever hold fast the blessed hope of everlasting life, he will not go far astray.

There is no danger that the parson will forget

that he is " in the world," but it is entirely possible for him not to be " of the world," so far as being influenced to the detriment of his work by its motive and spirit. There is much in the world which is beautiful and worthy of our love and admiration. The spirit of the world to-day is a very different spirit from that which prevailed before the advent of Christianity. Nevertheless it is true that there is an attitude towards life and conduct, often discernible, which can only be described as " worldly " in the reprehensible sense. This is more easily felt than described, but it soon becomes evident to the community in which a minister lives and it is soon discovered whether he is a man animated by the highest motives or is governed by lower ideals. One is sometimes rather startled to see how quickly a community takes the measure of a man, and also how accurate, as a general rule, their verdict is. Moreover, of all men in the community, perhaps no one is more closely observed than the clergyman. His sacred office will not secure for him immunity from such critical judgment, and indeed, may rather invite it. It is fatal for the minister to imagine that any affectation of priestly authority which he may assume, will take him out of the category of ordinary human standards. He is a house set on a hill, to be observed of all men. It is the man behind the office, after all, which really counts, and if, in all his relations, private, domestic, social, ecclesiastical, financial, he recommends himself as one whose life is in harmony with his profession, that conclusion will have been reached because of the character of the man, and not on account of his cloth.

Therefore, as one's influence for good depends so entirely on what a man really is, how important that one's outward conduct should be but the simple expression of one's inner and overmastering convictions.

If, thus far, we have dwelt upon the value of character, molded by the influence of Christian love, it is not to widen the distance between a minister and his people, but rather to bring them more closely together. For his greatest efficiency as a spiritual leader, he should be intimately identified with his flock, in their joys and sorrows, in their worldly ambitions and achievements, in all that makes for their religious and social betterment. So far as is possible, he should sink his official self-complacency in an earnest desire to be of service wherever an opportunity presents itself. It is always a misfortune for the clergy to become a distinct class in society. It was because they had assumed such aloofness of attitude in his day that the famous Sydney Smith was led to remark sarcastically, that there were three sexes in the world, men, women, and parsons. In our own communion, a man's clerical dress generally marks him out as a minister. There are clergymen who affect the attire of the ordinary business man, sincerely feeling, no doubt, that thus they can get nearer to their people and break down the reserve so often felt on the part of people in their contact with their minister. But this is a vain conceit, and really deceives no one, while it often exposes a clergyman to embarrassing situations. Men instinctively respect a person who is not ashamed of his calling, whatever it may be. There is an obvious propriety in the soldier wearing the uniform of his country. It both helps the soldier to remember his duty to his flag, and commands for him the consideration that is his due. It is rather painful, therefore, to see a clergyman, however worthy may be his intentions, appearing before the world in non-clerical attire. It seldom, if ever, leads to any good result. Of course these remarks do not apply, we need hardly say, to a man who is on vacation, and for purposes of comfort or economy doffs his clerical dress as one would naturally when playing golf or fishing or hunting. But while it is not desirable, even if it were possible, for a man to hide his office, it is equally reprehensible to allow the office to hide the man, or to make the man an object of dread to society, or an incubus on the natural flow and buoyancy of young life. It is always a bad sign to see young people take to their heels when they see the parson coming. The genial presence of the beloved shepherd of the flock should be welcome in any gathering of his people. Where this is not true, we may be sure it is a reflection, either on the character of the minister, or the people themselves. Of course it is not always easy to maintain the balance between a too easy-going familiarity and an unnecessary affectation of professional dignity.

Bishop Alonzo Potter, at one time the great Bishop of Pennsylvania, used to recount an incident of his own experience which also reflected a significant sidelight on one of his clergy. The Bishop himself was a man of great reserve and few words, and of a rather severe outward demeanor. It seems that on one occasion, he was being driven to a country church by a rather notorious horse jockey, who was asked by his rector to meet the Diocesan at the station. The Bishop had been brought up on a farm and was a good judge of a horse. This knowledge soon became evident to his driver, and established between the two men a spirit of cordial comradery. As they drove along, the voluble jockey said, " Well, Bishop, you have sent us a fine parson this time. Why, our preacher is a hustler.

He can do anything. He raises pigs and chickens, keeps a cow, has a fine garden, and is one of them fine fellers what everybody likes. He is jolly and sociable like, and pats you on the back like a real man. Of course he ain't got no more religion than you nor me."

The parson's home life ought to be an example for the people to follow, as he promised in his ordination vow to try to make it. He cannot do this if he marries unwisely. We have sometimes wished that the ordination service might contain two more questions, one of which should be, " Will you promise not to marry for five years after your ordination? " The other might well be, " Will you promise to answer letters promptly? " This latter question should also be among those asked at the consecration of every Bishop. But the early and ill-advised marriages of our young clergy, are often a positive and pathetic calamity, as we can testify, after a wide observation extending over many years. There are of course many glorious exceptions, as we are only too happy to affirm. But it is a fact that no sane young man of the world, looking forward to a business career, as a Doctor, Lawyer, Engineer, or Merchant, will embarrass his future, and bring inevitable distress upon his little family by embarking upon the matrimonial sea until his place in the business world is at least fairly assured, and his salary adequate to support, albeit modestly, those who may be dependent on him. On the contrary he will wait and work, till he can, with a manly self-respect, ask some young woman to share his fate and fortune. But in the church, marriage seems to follow ordination almost immediately, salary or no salary. The sad part of it is, that it often happens that the young cleric has allowed himself to become engaged to some young school girl or friend of his youth, and while he has been to the University and Seminary, and had the advantage of coming in contact with varied means of culture, his future wife has had but meager opportunities for intellectual or social development. The two young people have simply grown away from each other. The result is, the man's happiness and future influence as a leader suffer irreparable loss.

We believe strongly in a married clergy and in thousands of instances a parson's success can be traced directly to the uplifting influence of a wise and devoted wife. In our Mother Church of England, there are innumerable instances where the country parsonages have been the nursery of the very finest type of consecrated Christian manhood and womanhood. Normally every young clergyman should look forward to a happy home and family. But for the sake of his great work, and those who must share his success or failure, let him wait till he has earned for himself a good report and proven by his work successfully performed, his ability to support a family. He will by that time have acquired a judgment and common sense which will enable him to choose a real helpmeet.

The parson owes a duty to society and in the discharge of that duty, well conceived, he may greatly increase his efficiency. But it is pitiable for him to try to shine as a social leader and such an aim on his part is sure to bring him and his work into deserved contempt and ridicule. Whether a minister be married or single, he cannot be too particular to avoid all occasion of just criticism in his relation with women. A flirt is always contemptible, but such a spirit when found in a clergyman is most reprehensible and will soon destroy his influence for good. It is important, therefore, not only to avoid the evil thing itself, but all appearance thereof. This cannot be successfully done without the exercise of care and sane judgment. Try and realize that there is nothing hidden in your life among the people, which shall not sooner or later be revealed and that your movements and all that you do are sure to be seen and known of all men.

We come now to the parson's recreations. His parish visits will ordinarily give him an abundance of fresh air and bodily exercise, especially if his people are scattered over a more or less extended area. If he is fortunate enough to have a horse and buggy, or a motor car, this will supply another means of being out of doors, and at the same time, of getting around among his people. If he enjoys playing tennis, this game will bring him in contact with many of his younger members, and will yield a harvest of vigorous and active physical exercise. Where a golf course is within reach, this ancient and royal game will afford a fascinating source of entertainment, during which all the trials and vexations and discouragements of the parish will be quite forgotten. Moreover, in this game, the worse you play, the more exercise you get, and one can play it with enjoyment long after he has reached the limit of three score years and ten. But whatever form it may assume, we cannot too strongly remind the parson that the relaxation of mind and spirit, which comes from being out in the open air, is most necessary if he would do his best work and maintain a high standard of acceptable service in ministering to his people.

If all other resources fail him, let him remember that nothing is better than a good long brisk walk, which is nearly always possible, and can be enjoyed even when the elements are not propitious. Let the parson remember, "that a merry heart doeth good like a medicine," and that next to holiness of life, there is perhaps no more valuable asset for the minister of Christ than a cheerful spirit.

The relation between the parson and his people, when based upon that mutual respect and affection which has grown up after years of faithful service, is one of the most beautiful and soul-satisfying that can be perceived. In the checkered vicissitudes in the lives of his people, young and old, as he has fed them, they have learned to love and trust him as the good shepherd. He has gone in and out before them, and the sheep have followed him for they have learned to know his voice. They are assured that he has come to give to them life, and to give it them more abundantly.

XII

THE PARSON AND HIS VESTRY

In our American branch of the church catholic, the secular or temporal affairs of the parish are committed to a body of men known as the vestry. Their number varies according to the size of the parish and is generally determined by the provisions of the charter under which the parish is organized, ranging from five to thirteen, more or less.

The vestry is elected by the votes of the congregation, and holds office for one year. Unless expressly forbidden by the charter, all vestrymen are eligible to reëlection each year, and frequently the personnel of the vestry changes but little from time to time. In the majority of parishes it is provided that the annual meeting for the election of Wardens and vestrymen shall take place Easter Monday of each year. At this annual meeting, it is the canonical right of the rector to preside, as well as at every meeting of the vestry.

In every self-supporting parish, it is the prerogative of the vestry to fill the office of rector whenever a vacancy shall occur. In some dioceses before the call is canonical and legal, the Bishop of the Diocese must be informed as to the name of the person whom it is proposed to call, and sufficient time allowed him in which to register his judgment as to the wisdom and fitness of their proposed choice. It would be well for every rector to assure himself that the call extended to him has been made with due observance of all canonical regulations before he accepts.

Among the duties devolving upon the vestry, the following may be mentioned. They are to serve as careful custodians of the church property, and especially to see that all the buildings belonging to the parish are kept in good repair, and the grounds neat and in order; also that all risk from fire be adequately covered by insurance. They are to employ a proper church sexton to attend to all the duties appertaining to that functionary, including the ringing of the bells at the hours of divine service. They are responsible for the prompt payment of all financial obligations incurred by the parish, of whatever kind, and especially to make generous provision for the support and physical comfort of the rector, that he may be entirely free from all financial anxiety, and thus enabled to give himself entirely to the spiritual work of his sacred office.

But if the vestry is thus under bounden obligation to discharge these and other kindred offices for the parish and its rector, the parson must not forget that he owes certain considerations to his vestry. It will be our aim in this chapter to dwell somewhat on the mutual relations of rector and vestry, and to specify some of the prerogatives of each, and the limitations provided by the church's law for the harmonious regulation of the affairs of the parish.

To begin with, then, we have already reminded the parson that the function of the vestry is to concern itself entirely with temporal affairs;

and we have mentioned a few of the interests committed to its care. It is equally important for the parson to remember that he is responsible solely for things spiritual within the parish. To specify a few of his duties, we might suggest that it falls to his office, and belongs to him exclusively, to give orders as to the hours when the various public services shall take place; to select the hymns and anthems to be sung in church, and to appoint the organist, choir master, and all the members of the choir, either directly or through the agency of some one to whom he has delegated this responsibility; to decide what character of ritual shall prevail in the church, whether more or less simple or ornate. If a curate or more is to be provided, it is his privilege alone to appoint him. It is his function to preach to the congregation, and no one but himself has the right to occupy his pulpit, save on invitation. To him is committed the entire management of the Sunday school. Should there be a superintendent, such officer is supposed to be appointed by him as well as those who act as teachers in the school. He is to officiate at all marriages, baptisms, funerals, confirmations, and other sacerdotal functions. Of course he can delegate any of these duties to his curate, or other minister, should he for any good reason desire to do so.

It will be seen from this partial enumeration of the duties of parson and vestry respectively, that they are quite distinct, and, when understood, there should not be any confusion or interference one with the other in their performance. But the real difficulty arises from the fact that, in so many instances, either vestry or parson, and sometimes both, are unfamiliar with the law which should govern them.

On the other hand, the rector is quite as likely to lose sight of the fact that everything that appertains to the material fabric of the church, such as the church furniture, stained glass windows, ornaments of the altar or sanctuary, belongs to the jurisdiction of the vestry and when any change or addition is contemplated consent of the vestry must first be obtained. In so trivial a matter as the placing of eucharistic or vesper lights on the altar by the rector, we have known congregations to be sadly divided, and most unhappy results to follow. The rector was anxious to add these ornaments, and perhaps a number of his people were in full sympathy with his desire. He has therefore unwittingly taken the law into his own hands, and made the change. He has done so, generally, quite unaware of the fact that such introduction was the sole prerogative of the vestry whose rights he has infringed upon and ignored. If, in such cases, the rector is familiar with his limitations, and will patiently and lovingly abide his time, and confer freely with his brethren of the vestry, he will nearly always find that his object can be accomplished and all friction avoided.

There is always a reasonable and an unreasonable, a right and a wrong way, to accomplish any given object. It is never wise to attempt to achieve our object by indirection.

So again with the matter of ritual and ceremony in the conduct of the services. The law of the church commits to the rector the entire control of the public worship. Moreover, the rubrics as well as the established custom of the church allow great variety in the matter of form and ceremony. By long established tradition, certain dioceses and individual parishes are accustomed to a more simple service than we find in others. People are frequently opposed to any radical departure from that to which by long use, they have been accustomed. When a vestry calls a clergyman as its rector, it naturally aims to secure a man who will carry on the services in the same manner they have learned to love, and the congregation they represent are quick to resent what they regard as innovations. Many a parish has been rent in twain, and unspeakable loss and injury have resulted through the indiscretion of young clergymen who have introduced forms and ceremonies distasteful, because unfamiliar, to the people. It may be that in thus acting, the clergyman is entirely within his canonical rights, for he and not the vestry or the people, has the sole authority to decide all such questions. But simply because the man has the power and authority to disturb the peace of a happy and united flock, is no reason whatever that he should exercise that right. There is a law of charity and common sense, as well as the law established by the canons. Surely when the church commits to her clergy the sacred responsibility of determining the ritual of God's Service she assumes that they will exercise it wisely, and with tender consideration for the consciences of their people.

Many of the questions which cause unrest and disquiet are not so much questions of the clergyman's rights as of his duty. Where mere matters of taste and not of any vital principles are concerned, a kind heart and a level head will generally lead the parson to put himself in the place of those who sit in the pews and thus enter into their feelings and sympathize with their preferences. He may be perfectly sure that wherever real principles are involved, for which valid and substantial reasons can be given, his people will in time come to agree with him. But nothing but harm to any good cause can result from ruthlessly disregarding the susceptibilities of those who cannot see things exactly from our point of view. It will therefore be the part of wisdom for the clergyman always to take his vestry into his confidence whenever he is contemplating any decided change in the realm of ritual or ceremony. They will be more willing and ready to recognize his authority, if he does not exercise it arbitrarily in utter disregard of their judgment. Here, if anywhere, the admirable tact and diplomacy of St. Paul will come to our relief. He says, "All things are lawful for me, but all things are not expedient; all things are lawful for me, but all things edify not. Let no man seek his own way, but every man another's good."

Happily the church has safely weathered the storms and controversies which were wont to rage about ritualistic practices not many years ago. One net result of the many battles that have been fought over such questions is that men are far more tolerant and broadminded in their judgments than formerly. There has surely emerged out of the conflict a strong conviction that any church which claims to be adapted to the needs of all sorts and conditions of men should be comprehensive enough to give welcome and hospitality to a great variety of ceremony.

" In essentials unity; in non-essentials liberty; in all things charity," is an ancient aphorism which has become more and more the guiding principle of the church's life and work.

When we contrast the dignity, reverence and beauty with which our church services are now almost universally conducted, with the careless and slovenly unseemliness of other days, we may well be thankful for the change that has taken place.

Moreover, in the presence of so many profound and anxious problems clamoring for solution, the church of to-day has caught a vision of her real mission in the world, and is no longer content to waste her energies on matters of mere æsthetic taste and individual preference. Quite irrespective of ecclesiastical parties and doctrinal differences, there is evidently a desire that all things be done decently and in order, according to St. Paul's wise maxim. While great liberty is allowed in the matter of rendering the services, it is not a liberty which seeks to violate the law, but a liberty which recognizes those limitations which safe-guard the church against unbridled license.

It is only as the parson is careful to familiarize himself with the prerogatives and duties of his vestry as well as his own, and accustoms himself to respect them, that he may reasonably hope that his own privileges and official position will be held in honor and esteem.

XIII

THE PARSON AND HIS CHOIR

We do not write as an expert in music, but rather as one who knows little or nothing about the divine art of song. Our simple aim in this chapter is to make some practical suggestions to the parson as to his relations to that important and indispensable adjunct of public worship known as the choir. The choir may be, and in the majority of cases we are glad to believe is, a comfort and blessing to the parson. In some instances, however, choirs have become the cause of most unhappy irritation in the congregation, and a source of vexation and heart-break to the parson. If we can make even a slight contribution towards the avoidance of misunderstanding between the parson and his choir, we shall not have written altogether in vain.

In the first place, then, let the parson try to realize that whether his choir is paid or purely voluntary, its members are entitled to his kindly and sympathetic consideration. Like himself, they occupy a conspicuous and often unenviable position. Whether they discharge their functions well or indifferently they are sure to be criticised. It may be fairly assumed that they are more or less eager and desirous to please the congregation, and to render an acceptable service. Surely then, the parson ought to be the first to pay them the tribute of courteous and grateful appreciation. He should sympathize with the sentiment of the cowboys on the plains who posted a large placard over the little melodeon with these words inscribed upon it. "Boys, please don't shoot the choir; they are doing their level best." Assuming that the parson maintains towards his choir this attitude of kindly consideration and steadfastly adheres to it, he is in a frame of mind to get the best results out of his choir. Being sure of his confidence and esteem, they will be most eager to please him and carry out his wishes.

If the parson is not conversant with music, he

will have to find in his congregation, or in the community, those who can assist him, thus forming the best available choir. If the choir is a paid one, the selection of those who constitute it is generally left to the choir-master, who may or may not be also the organist. Should the choir be a voluntary one, he will be fortunate if he can find an efficient and conscientious man or woman in the congregation, willing to become responsible for the recruiting and the training of the singers. In country parishes, the problem of the organist and the choir often becomes a critical one, and calls for the exercise of great tact, patience, and common sense on the part of the minister. There is little or no money to pay salaries to those who help in this part of the service. It is all a labor of love on the part of a few faithful people, who can sing, and are willing to give their services freely. But whatever the nature of the choir, whether paid or free, the parson must not forget that the church by the enactment of canon 25, has made him entirely responsible in the matter of the church music.

THE PARSON AND HIS CHOIR

By this canon, it is made the duty of the minister, either by standing directions, or from time to time, to appoint such hymns or anthems as are to be sung. It is also made his duty, with such assistance as he may see fit to employ, from persons skilled in music, to give orders concerning the tunes to be sung at any time in his church; and especially it shall be his duty to suppress all light and unseemly music, and all indecency and irreverence in the performance by which vain and ungodly persons profane the service of the sanctuary.

This canon is printed in full on a front page of every copy of the authorized hymnal, for the information and guidance of both minister and choir, and all others concerned. Notwithstanding the publicity given this canon, there are many clergymen, strange to say, and far more people, who are not even aware of its existence. We have been appealed to as Bishop, many times, by ministers as well as congregations, to settle questions which have arisen in connection with the choir, whereas even a cursory acquaintance with the canonical law, accessible at all times, would have made any such controversy impossible.

Therefore, we draw especial attention to the canon now, that the parson may fully understand both the authority and responsibility committed to him by the church's law with regard to his choir. He is absolutely the court of final appeal on all questions appertaining to the personnel of the choir and the music to be sung. The canon places the settlement of all questions which may arise in the hands of the parson. But while this authority has been wisely vested in him, the minister has the right to assign and delegate it to others, and thus relieve himself of many details, while often securing at the same time better results.

Inasmuch as among other religious bodies by which we are surrounded, full authority is not always thus given to the minister, it would be wise, in order to avoid all possible misunderstanding, for him, from time to time, in meeting with his choir, to thank them for their valuable services and remind them that while the church has given him full authority to appoint all the members of the choir and select the tunes, he is most grateful that these duties have been so cheerfully and satisfactorily performed by others whom he has asked to act for him.

Conditions vary so greatly in different parishes that no uniform rules can be made to apply in all cases. In the smaller parishes where those who form the choir, give their services, it will often be found desirable, if not necessary, for the parson to be present at the weekly rehearsals if only to show his keen interest and appreciation.

The question of vesting the choir has happily ceased, in most places at least, to be one involving any disturbing elements. The conviction has gradually become almost universal, that where it can be secured, a seemly and appropriate uniform for the choir is a decided gain, indeed, vested choirs are frequently found nowadays in other churches than those of our own communion. Care should be taken that in the case of women an Oxford cap, or other suitable head-covering, be provided, and that for both sexes, a simple cotta and cassock be worn, thus securing uniformity. It is very unseemly, and in exceedingly bad taste, to see different colored skirts appearing below the cottas. We have been surprised to find that some clergymen allowed such a departure from the evident fitness of things, for no matter how poor a parish is, there is always some way of providing a decent vestment for the boys and girls when the effort is made.

The advent of the vested boy choir a number of years ago ushered in a new era in our church music. The norm in the great majority of our churches, when able to provide it, is now a choir composed entirely of men and boys. It has been found that, when properly trained by a competent choir master, the employment of boys' voices has added greatly to the sweetness and melody of the music. Quite aside from the very great contribution which the introduction of boys' voices has made to our musical enrichment the moral and religious influence of this widely spread movement upon thousands of our boys has proven a by-product of incalculable value. The boy himself, being thus brought into close personal contact with his rector, and those occupied with endeavoring to make the service of praise acceptable to God, being trained Sunday after Sunday in the public worship of the church, to habits of reverence and decorum, educated to take his part in the prayers and songs of the church, almost necessarily derives great spiritual help from his long connection with the choir. He is at least placed in an environment where wholesome influences of the highest educational value surround him. One cannot wonder, therefore, that hundreds of our very best laymen to-day, trace back their first impressions of the church to the days, when, as boys, they sang in the choir; while the instances are by no means few where young men have become candidates for the holy ministry through the same influence. The boy choir has really become a fruitful nursery for the recruiting of the ranks of the ministry itself.

The possibility of thus influencing for good the lives of boys, and molding their future usefulness, is an inspiration to the wise parson to do all he can for such boys. It is of prime importance that the organist himself should be a Christian gentleman of clean, manly, and devoted life, and that the choir master, before he is employed, should give absolute proof of a high Christian character.

The parson will seek frequent opportunity to encourage his young choristers in their good work, and an occasional outing for their special delectation, or some other form of recreation, will be an investment which will surely bring forth salutary results in attaching these young Christian soldiers more loyally to the church.

As before intimated, we do not deem ourselves competent to embark upon the discussion of the various kinds of music to be sung. Happily this duty does not lend itself to the purpose of these suggestions which aim to be entirely practical in their character. Moreover, the canon on church music, to which we have already referred, warns the parson that it is his duty to suppress all light and unseemly music.

THE PARSON AND HIS CHOIR

There are certain clear and explicit limitations set forth in the canon as to the quality of music to be sung. The hymns, for instance, must be such as are set forth by authority, that is, they must be contained in our authorized hymnal. In the matter of anthems, only those are to be sung which are in the words of holy scripture. If these simple rules govern the parson, his choir will not go far astray.

If we may here put in a plea for the poor choir-afflicted, and musically persecuted Bishop, we should like to whisper to the parson, " Do not let the choir spread itself too freely, and soar too high, when he comes for confirmation." There is a great temptation on such an occasion to try to impress the Bishop with the superior excellence of the choir, and to show him what they are capable of doing. We believe we speak for many Bishops besides ourselves, when we say, " Please give us a simple service, plain chants, and familiar hymns." Now and then it will do no harm to have some other processional than " Onward, Christian Soldiers," inspiring as it may be.

Give that grand old hymn a rest occasionally.

A greatly beloved brother Bishop of ours was wont to say, " I am nearly worn out. I have had to go day after day in my rounds of the parishes from a big turkey dinner to the ' Church's one Foundation.' "

As to singing anthems not in the words of holy scripture, it was recently our experience to officiate in the church of a little country town, where visitors from the city were accustomed to spend the summer. The young candidate for holy orders, whom we had appointed to take charge of the services there, found more or less difficulty in recruiting his choir. On the occasion of our visitation, the church was filled to its utmost capacity, with people standing in the aisles. At the Offertory, two young women from the city had volunteered to sing an anthem. They were sisters, members of another religious body, and not familiar with our customs. They gave us, in a manner that made the performance forever memorable, a love song, with an interminable number of verses, every one of which ended, "Goodnight, goodnight, beloved." Of course the young man had not taken the precaution to ask them what they proposed to sing. It is needless to say, if that was not his first, it will probably be his last offense in that particular direction.

It is in the matter of the anthems, where the canon is most frequently ignored, and where the most painful and outrageous violations of good taste and religious propriety are perpetrated. It will cost a few cents more, but it will be money well spent, if the parson will consult some well informed brother clergyman, or churchly choirmaster, in a sister parish, and get the address of the publisher of such anthems as are worthy to be sung in the house of God. But let the parson avoid the cheap and popular song books, so often used in our churches, in utter disregard of the church's authority.

When one considers what a very prominent place the musical feature occupies in our services, as prescribed by the book of common prayer, it seems strange that more attention has not been paid to the musical education of our clergy.

The parts of the service, including the Psalter, which are supposed to be sung, comprise a large element of the whole. Such is not the case in the public worship of any of the Protestant bodies around us. With them, frequently, a few hymns and an occasional anthem are all that are demanded. In our service, versicles, various responses, canticles, chants, the Te Deum, the Psalter, and other features call for musical rendition.

Would it not be well if a chair of music were established in every theological seminary? Even where a student for the ministry possesses little or no natural gift for music, he could be taught how to read the notes and the simple elements of the art. To be able, when occasion demanded it, to sit down at the organ and play a familiar hymn or chant would be a valuable asset in the equipment of every clergyman for his work. There are very few voices that, with a little training, cannot carry a simple tune, and thus lead the singing in services held in school houses, mission halls, or country churches. Even such elementary knowledge would enable the parson to be of great service to his choir and increase his efficiency.

The function of music in the worship of God is so vital and fundamental that the church has always recognized its value both in the old and new dispensations. The worship of the temple at Jerusalem, when that historical fane was consecrated, reminds us that, " The trumpeters and singers made one sound to be heard in praising and thanking the Lord "; and the book of Revelation speaks of a " Voice from Heaven, as the voice of many waters, and as the voice of a great thunder, and the voice of harpers, harping with their harps." In all the ages of the past, it has been through music that the religious emotions of men have found their highest and most articulate expression. No one can estimate what a debt of gratitude the Christian world owes the great composers and masters of classic music, who, in operas and masses, and sacred song, have with rare genius interpreted to multitudes the spirit of our holy religion.

A BISHOP'S MESSAGE

Numerous instances have been recorded of great crowds being molded as one man under the spell of some national air, while the psychological effect of a popular hymn on the religious susceptibilities of a congregation, is a matter of common observation.

XIV

THE PARSON AND HIS SUNDAY SCHOOL

The day has happily gone by when the parson can afford to regard his Sunday School, either as an inevitable nuisance, or as a comparatively insignificant part of his work.

It is now everywhere recognized that his influence among the boys and girls of his flock, tells vitally on the life and growth of the parish. When a vacant parish is looking around for a desirable rector, one of the first questions asked about any possible choice is, " Is he a good Sunday School man? " " Does he take a personal interest in the children? " and " Is he fond of the young people? "

One of the most encouraging marks of modern church life is the vastly increased emphasis it is placing upon everything that concerns the Christian education of the child. Just as, in the public schools of our country, pedagogy is being reduced to an exact science, and methods of child culture have provided for the young every advantage that psychology could suggest, so in our church schools men are devoting their lives to giving our children the best advantages that modern scholarship can discover. In our own church, the General Board of Religious Education has adopted a standard curriculum based upon the most approved modern methods, and provincial and diocesan boards of religious education coördinating with this general board are doing all in their power to make it effective. In the Sunday schools, now called church schools, it is verily true that old things are passing away, and behold all things are becoming new.

It has been the aim of this General Board of Religious Education to determine, first of all, what a child ought to be taught through the church school, then to recommend the most scientific methods of imparting that knowledge. As a means to this end, it has been recognized as never before, that in the proper training and equipment of the teachers themselves lies the key to all true and worthy success. For our great encouragement, we can see on every hand that no subject is commanding more attention in the church today and none gives promise of a richer and more beneficent harvest. It is quite true that there are parsons who are not as yet fully awakened to the importance of this movement, and lag behind their brethren, and would fain impede the way of progress. But their tribe is diminishing, and is destined to be swept away in the strong current which is carrying the best thought of the modern church along with it. Abundant and most timely literature is teeming from the press, illustrative of child nurture, and the subject is so presented as to invest the whole discussion with picturesque and lively interest.

In nearly all our Theological Seminaries, chairs of religious pedagogy are being established and endowed, in order that the art of inculcating in the mind of our youth the saving truths of our holy religion may form a prominent part in the curriculum and be made a pre-requisite for ordination.

The time has come when an applicant for a position as teacher in our public schools has but meager chance of appointment unless he is a graduate of a normal college, where the teacher is taught the art of imparting his knowledge. Similarly, teacher training schools are being formed for our church school teachers where modern methods are explained, and summer schools are held in many dioceses, in which interesting lectures on teacher training are systematically given.

All this well-regulated activity and quickened interest mean that the parson of the future must be well equipped to lead and inspire his teachers, and hence must be well taught himself.

It is a trite saying that the Sunday School is the nursery of the church of the future, and that on the quality of the instruction given depends, in a large measure, the character of the Christian citizenship of our country. Well authenticated statistics have shown us again and again that men and women, who are allowed to reach adult age, without being brought into personal allegiance to Christ and made members of His church, rarely become active Christians afterwards. It is during the tender and susceptible years of childhood and youth, that deep impressions are made, and the foundation of Christian character well established.

All these considerations point to the unique opportunity the parson enjoys of molding, by his example and wisely directed efforts, the lives committed to his care. It is not strange that occasionally young men called to the ministry have no great love for children, and possess but little natural aptitude for teaching. While either one of these limitations is a serious disqualification for successful work, they need not prove an insuperable barrier. It is the bounden duty of the parson to cultivate by every possible means that faculty with which by nature he has not been endowed. No effort in this direction will be misspent, and most excellent books are at his command, written for the express purpose of helping him to overcome these very obstacles. Let the parson pray earnestly for such a passion for the souls of Christ's little ones, that he will be able to avail himself of every opportunity to learn the art of winning them. Here as elsewhere, love begets love, and he will soon find that no part of his sacred calling gives a more real delight and pleasure than securing their confidence.

It will be of great advantage to the parson, if he will take pains to know the children personally in their homes, and thus break down that shyness and reserve with which young people are so frequently disposed to regard their minister. To recognize them when they meet on the street, and to greet them by name with a cheerful word and smile, will have its wholesome effect.

In this connection, we would like to urge the parson, most earnestly, to remember that he cannot, save at his own peril and real loss to the children, relegate the care of the Sunday School altogether, either to his curate or to his lay-superintendent, however well equipped they may be. We have observed that this is not infrequently done by well meaning and worthy pastors. But it is a serious mistake. We realize that the reason given is that the rector is so busy and has so many important matters to occupy his mind, that he can ill afford to spare the time to be with the children. But the children soon draw their own conclusions as to their relative importance in their minister's eyes, and he thus loses the precious opportunity to influence and help the lambs of his flock.

It ought to be regarded as a sacred duty, never to be neglected, at least to show himself and briefly to greet every class and its teacher on Sunday.

The act of publicly catechizing the children of his school is made a plain duty incumbent upon every priest. To learn to do this skillfully and in such wise as to hold the interest of the children, and at the same time thoroughly indoctrinate them in those truths which every Christian should know to his soul's health, is a most worthy and valuable achievement. Such a practice also gives the priest an excellent opportunity to instruct the younger members of his flock, as well as children of a larger growth who may be present, in many things not suggested by the catechism, but nevertheless well worth while.

We have already referred to the emphasis laid to-day on teacher training. The parson will not fail to organize his church school teachers into classes and meet them regularly for instruction and inspiration. We are persuaded that the difficulty which confronts so many rectors in securing teachers for their schools is chiefly due to a feeling of incompetence on the part of those asked to give themselves to this work. It would therefore be well for the minister, if he could have always in process of training, a normal class of young people, with the view of adequately supplying this need of well instructed teachers. By this means, as teachers dropped out, he would have a source of supply from which he could select proper persons to instruct his young people.

There is one more opportunity of great service which the rector enjoys in connection with his Sunday School. We refer to that of seeking out and encouraging the brightest and best of his boys to consider the claims of the holy ministry. Were this privilege made use of more frequently, and young men well endowed by nature and grace, brought face to face with the question, " Why should I not devote my life to the service of my fellowmen in the work of the ministry?" we confidently believe many more would find that high vocation. The Holy Spirit operates through human agency and men have ever been influenced to the highest and noblest endeavor through some word or good example from their fellowmen. If, in the impressionable days of their youth, before they have fully settled the question of their life-work, men are thus reminded of the opportunity for heroism, self-sacrifice, and devotion awaiting them in this greatest of all fields of service for God and man, many will be ready to respond. The Sunday school offers an unique opportunity to the parson thus to lead young men to make such self-surrender in a spirit of manly consecration.

The parson should frequently ask himself what,

177

after all, is the ultimate aim of the Sunday school so far as the individual child is concerned? Is it not to implant such knowledge of the life and teaching of Christ as may lead the young mind to love Him more and more? Religion must be so presented as to be attractive and induce the child to desire to know more of its charm and beauty. To this end the church school should be a place, which by its atmosphere, and environment, appeals to the boy or girl. Short and hearty services in which all can take part, bright and inspiring hymns, such as all can join in singing, and the whole session brought easily within an hour's time so as not to weary the child, should be the prevailing custom. Everything should be prepared beforehand and the service should be rendered with life and animation.

Then, as the child is being trained to take his place in the church as an intelligent and earnest Christian man, he should be taught by object lessons, to be familiar with the various offices and sacramental rites of the church, and their spiritual meaning. Care should be taken that he should witness the administration of holy baptism, in which he himself, as a child, was made a member of Christ, a child of God, and an inheritor of the Kingdom of Heaven.

The whole school should be brought from time to time into the body of the church when some of its members, or others, are to be baptized. Then also at the time of the Bishop's visitation for confirmation, the presence of the children should be encouraged. It is highly desirable also that either by means of children's communion services, or otherwise, every child old enough to understand, should have the great privilege from time to time of witnessing, as a worshiper, the reverent and devout celebration of the Holy Eucharist. In all these experiences, the child's mind and heart are informed and made sympathetically intelligent as to the great means of grace.

Moreover, as respect and a wholesome awe for the house of God is so essential to the growth of the religious spirit, the parson should not fail to inculcate by every possible means, a deep sense of reverence for the church building and all within it. The practice of silence within the sacred edifice, or speaking in a subdued tone, should become almost instinctive with the child.

It is also a helpful and edifying custom, when the school is brought into the church, to describe occasionally, with reverent and painstaking particularity, the furniture of the sanctuary and chancel and other parts of the church. The parson should point out, calling each by its name, the several parts. At the same time the reverence due the altar, the significance of the ornaments thereon, the use of the credence, prayer desk, lectern, pulpit, chancel-rail, can all be dwelt upon. Such a lesson, repeated as occasion offers, will be not only interesting, but highly instructive to the child. Thus the place where God's honor dwelleth will become more and more dear and sacred to the young soul and he will think of it as none other than the house of God and the gate of Heaven.

XV

THE PARSON CONDUCTING PUBLIC WORSHIP

Twice on Sunday, and often during the week, the parson appears before the people as the leader of their devotions.

On these solemn occasions, how vitally important it is, both for the parson and his people, that all things be done as St. Paul suggests decently and in order. The first pre-requisite of an edifying public worship is that a genuinely religious atmosphere should be created. To achieve this happy result, so much depends on the minister himself, that it will be well worth our effort to consider how he may best contribute to it.

We venture to mention first the element of promptness as to the time of beginning and ending his service. It is not always easy to accomplish this, especially in country parishes, where people have to do their own work, and perhaps live at a remote distance from the church. But all obstacles of this kind can be overcome, if the minister only realizes the value of time, and what a vital part it plays in the religious life. A congregation can be gradually trained to expect that at the appointed hour the service will begin. If he makes it a matter of conscientious duty to be in his place on time, the organist and choir will soon learn that they must observe the same rule and the education of the congregation in the practice of punctuality will follow as a matter of course. A minister cannot be too persistent in observing this habit.

While the people are gathering for their devotions, great care should be taken to see that such reverential quiet and order be maintained as is seemly in the house of God. To secure this, it is only necessary that the minister himself be reverential and quiet; that is, that he should realize in his own mind and heart the nature of the great act in which he and his people are about to engage. He has come to lead them into the

182

conscious presence of the King of Kings and Lord of Lords, and the emotions which that thought will naturally enkindle will induce him to cultivate in manner and bearing a worshipful spirit. How often it happens that a light and flippant manner on the part of the minister before the service, leading him to indulge in trifling conversation with his people, utterly spoils the religious atmosphere of the place, and forfeits on the very threshold of our approach to God, the first condition of a prayerful and devoted spirit.

If such painful and distressing dissipation of a feeling of reverence may thus occur before the service begins, it is equally possible for the good effects of the service, otherwise helpful, to be ruined by what occurs after the service is concluded. If, when the benediction has been pronounced and the choir has withdrawn, and the amen has been sung, the people rise from their knees only to engage in loud and noisy conversation, the result is almost, if not quite, as unhappy. The people should depart from the House of God, as they enter it, quietly and reverently. This does not mean, necessarily that friends and neighbors should not greet each other with a look or word of kindly recognition, but simply that over the entire scene there should preside the impression, that with the blessing of peace resting upon them, the people should retire from the house of prayer with the religious sense deepened rather than driven away.

More than once we have seen the habit of loud talking, and behavior unbecoming the house of God, broken up by the manner of the minister himself without uttering a word of reproof. Returning from the Sacristy and proceeding to the church door where he was wont to greet the people passing out he would whisper deprecatingly as he moved through groups of them engaged in conversation. Immediately silence was restored as they understood from his bearing and quiet hushed demeanor, that such unintentional irreverence was entirely out of place. No incident could better illustrate the power and effect of a reverent manner on the part of the priest.

And now, assuming that this obvious attitude

184

on the part of the officiating minister and people has been secured before the service begins we are ready to consider the parson's part as a leader of the devotions of his people.

This brings us to the manner of reading the church service on which, it is admitted, on all hands, so much depends. On this subject so much has been written that one hesitates to enter upon its discussion. But we venture to remind the parson that no words of ours can possibly exaggerate the importance of a sincere, intelligent, impressive, and edifying, rendering of the church's tender, sympathetic and beautiful offices. It is easy to say, and obviously true, that the real preparation for a proper rendering of the church service takes place in the heart of the minister himself. Unless his own mind and spirit are obsessed with the reality and genuineness of the thoughts the church puts into his mouth, it can hardly be expected that he can bring home to the worshipers their significance. This means that the parson should not enter upon the performance of his sacred duty without finding time to ask

God in prayer to grant him the assistance of the Holy Spirit.

In the celebration of the holy communion, that greatest of all services, in which the priest has the privilege to engage, the very solemnity of the occasion generally safeguards it against irreverence. But even here there is often need to caution the minister against the appearance of undue haste, and remind him how exceedingly important it is that he should render with the greatest care every part of the divine office. It would be well if every young man about to be ordained to the priesthood, should learn from some one who knows, how to celebrate correctly. The disposition of the holy vessels, the preparation of the altar, the arrangement of the various linens, his manual acts and postures, all become important. The impressive and beautiful simplicity of our communion service can be so presented as to deeply affect the heart of the devout worshiper. In what we shall say here about reading the service, we shall address ourselves chiefly to the offices of morning and evening prayer.

The opening sentences can be so read as to recall the wandering thoughts of an entire congregation, and fix them upon the things of eternity. We have heard the exhortation read so impressively that its effect has been most solemnizing and uplifting. The tone and manner in which the priest leads the people in the general confession are capable of expressing the emotions of a truly penitent heart or just the opposite. Then the gracious words of the church's absolution, when pronounced in accordance with their intended meaning, can convey to the penitent infinite comfort and peace.

Indeed, the aim of the parson, throughout the entire service, should be to have his own spirit so attuned to the meaning of the sentiments expressed, that his rendition of them will fully interpret them to his hearers.

Important as all the service is, it is perhaps in the reading of the appointed lessons that the parson should especially endeavor to convey to his fellow-worshipers, distinctly and intelligently the significance of the message contained in the word of God.

The exasperating habit formed by so many of our younger clergy of racing through the various parts of the church service cannot be too severely condemned. Such a practice not only results in throwing away a great opportunity of helpful ministration placed at the parson's disposal, but frequently disgusts the devout worshiper, while alienating the careless and indifferent.

We speak from a long experience with all sorts and conditions of clergymen when we declare that no effort the parson can put forth will bring him a more sure reward, than that expended in learning to read the church service acceptably.

We should like to enter our protest here against the affectation of a sort of mechanical sing-song monotone, so frequently met with in those rendering the church service, and which emasculates it of all spiritual significance and approaches near to painful mummery. We do not refer to a dignified and proper intoning of the service, which in Cathedrals and large churches may be adopted with edification. Even here care should be taken that it be done well. We have in mind rather a sort of unnatural and perfunctory hurrying through the offices, even including the lessons, in a tone whose only merit is that the agony of those who must endure it will soon be over.

Good reading is an art which is not beyond the reach of the average parson to acquire, and one important requisite of it is that it should be natural. A man's common sense as to the fitness of things will indicate to him that he should not read a lesson of holy scripture or a prayer in the same tone and inflection as he would an article in a newspaper. But that does not mean that an affected clerical tone or manner should be employed. To convey the meaning of what is read, and to realize where and what we are reading are the chief requisites, nor must it be forgotten that the voice should be sustained at such a pitch as to make the reading easily audible.

In another chapter, we have spoken of the sermon, and here we would only add that care should be taken to deliver our message briefly, and when we have made our point and driven it home to the hearts of our people, to bring it to a close.

On one occasion, a parson asked his wife how she liked his sermon. She replied that there were several admirable places where he could have stopped to great advantage but he did not. It is certainly possible to preach a congregation into the right spirit and then out of it again. It is always well to bear in mind the physical and mental limitations of poor human nature, and it is wise even to err occasionally on the side of mercy. It is said that a certain distinguished preacher who was invited to address the students of Yale, asked President Hadley about how long he should preach. His rather memorable reply was, " Well, Doctor, we do not like to limit our preachers in such matters, but I have observed by long experience that not many souls are saved after twenty minutes."

For a young preacher learning the art, it will be wise to so prepare himself that he can bring his message within the compass of fifteen minutes. The late Dr. William R. Huntington, sometime rector of Grace Church, New York, when told by the chairman of the House of Deputies that he had only fifteen minutes to close a debate, involving issues of momentous importance, replied, " Thank you, Mr. Chairman, if a man cannot say what is in his mind in fifteen minutes he had better not speak at all."

In bringing this chapter to a close I shall venture to speak of the practical importance of ventilation in our churches, and of securing an abundance of fresh, pure air during the conduct of public worship. It is true that the modern church is more likely to have regard to this important requisite, than those of a former generation, but even now there is much to be desired in this respect. Many architects are strangely neglectful of such sanitary and hygienic precautions. The parson owes it to his own success and efficiency, as well as to the health and comfort of his people to see that this is not overlooked. The most eloquent sermon will fall flat, if the congregation is stupefied with the poison of a vitiated atmosphere.

The parson will also see that his church is kept

warm and comfortable, avoiding the extremes, both of heat and cold. It takes more religious enthusiasm than the modern Christian possesses to bring him a second time to a church where he has been chilled or has contracted a heavy cold. One such experience will last some people a life-time.

It may occur to the parson that all these matters concerning the church building being kept in a proper condition belong to the duties of the vestry. This is quite true theoretically, but if the parson is not back of his vestry to insist that these matters, so vital to the highest interests of public worship, are attended to, they will, as experience shows, often be neglected.

This chapter has dwelt on the parson conduct-ing public worship. Let us say that we have assumed all along that he has a congregation to which to minister. This assumption, however, will not always be a safe one in these days unless the parson has a message worth hearing, and moreover, the individuals who attend his church are made welcome when they reach the church door. Not only cold air, but cold and indifferent hearts will repel the stranger, and he will come no more. Even for the habitual worshiper, it is a pleasant experience to be met at the church door graciously and be shown to a good seat. But for a stranger, a smile of welcome, a cordial greeting, and some expression of human kindness extended means more than it is easy to describe.

The parson should see to it that ushers meet every worshiper and especially that the chance visitor is made to feel at home and provided with a prayer book and hymnal and invited to come again.

A failure to observe these simple amenities of Christian fellowship and ordinary civility has been the lamentable cause of serious criticism in many of our churches. For a church to get the reputation of snobbishness or of lacking in brotherly sympathy is fatal to its success.

XVI

THE PARSON AND THE INSTITU-
TIONAL CHURCH

A great awakening of parochial activity has taken place in the church within the memory of many of us still living. The direction in which this increased vitality has developed, on the whole, has been salutary and most commendable.

Those of us who are older, can recall the day when the only services held in the church were on Sunday morning and evening; the session of the Sunday school; and perhaps, during the week, an evening service on Wednesday or Friday, very poorly attended. The holy communion was celebrated as a rule, after morning prayer on the first Sunday in the month. The churches were generally locked up on Sunday night till the next Sunday, save when opened for the one evening service during the week.

THE INSTITUTIONAL CHURCH

There were few, if any, organizations of men or women engaged in church work of any kind.

We may well congratulate ourselves on the change that has taken place. To-day it is not at all unusual to find our church doors open at all times, inviting the devout to come in and rest and pray. Even the stranger passing by is often tempted to drop in and fall upon his knees for a few moments, for it is evident the church is a house of prayer for all people.

The holy communion, once celebrated monthly at mid-day, is now offered at an early hour every Sunday in the great majority of our churches, large and small, throughout the country, while in our Cathedrals, and not a few of our larger churches, there is a daily celebration attended by devout worshipers. Moreover, the offices of morning and evening prayer are recited daily in a constantly increasing number of parishes. These are only a few of the many evidences which might be given of the increased life of the church.

For all these proofs of genuine spiritual growth, we may well thank God and take courage.

A BISHOP'S MESSAGE

Along with this quickened appreciation, of the church's heritage of worship, there has also sprung up a vastly enlarged and almost bewildering number of organizations of almost every kind and description. So numerous are the guilds, brotherhoods, auxiliaries, missionary societies, leagues, and ladies' aids, in the average modern parish, that one actually wonders when the parson finds time in which to say his prayers, read his Bible, write his sermons, and cultivate his own spiritual life, that he may edify his people and minister to their needs.

Such a church as I have endeavored to describe is known as the Institutional Church, and while there are various degrees of intensity, of which the unfortunate rector finds himself a victim, the type is easily recognized and has become more or less universal.

While gratefully recognizing the advantages of a live parish as compared with a dead one of the old class, it must be admitted there are grave dangers to parson and people, connected with the new order.

For the parson himself, there is the obvious risk that such incessant demands on his time and strength will leave him little or no leisure for prayer and meditation. If, when so much of spiritual inspiration and uplift is going out of a man, his heart and soul are not constantly replenished day by day with the unction and grace of the Holy Spirit, which can only come by his being alone with God, unspeakable loss must ensue. A man can only preach what he has seen and felt. He must give out of his own abundance which God has poured into his heart, in order to supply the various and never-ceasing hunger of his people. If the supply of the oil of strength and gladness runs so low through lack of replenishment from the divine source that the parson's own lamp has gone out, how can the people who follow him see their way? A congregation is quick to discern the difference between the praying parson, and the man whose chief aim is simply professional success. The verdict of the people here is infallible.

Closely akin to this first and obvious danger,

arising from such preoccupation, is the impoverishment of the parson's intellectual life. At our ordination, we promise before the altar, not only to be diligent in prayers and in reading of the Holy Scriptures, but also in such studies as help to the knowledge of the same. We live in an age when the standard of popular education is becoming higher and higher. Men are reading and thinking as never before. The time has come when the only hope for the ministry to command and hold a place of real leadership and influence is through spiritual and intellectual equipment. At his own great peril, will the parson allow his time to be frittered away on all kinds of engagements and meetings to the utter neglect of reading and study. He is living in the twentieth century and the parson's sermons should give evidence that he is in touch with his environment and the age in which he lives. Not only the great books of the past are to be digested, but the helpful and inspiring books which are teeming from the press at the present day, will receive his careful consideration. His very position demands of him that he shall know what other men are reading and thinking about. He must be constantly bringing out of his treasury for the encouragement and guidance of his people, things both new and old. The parson who allows himself to go to seed, spiritually or intellectually, has betrayed his sacred trust and failed to keep his ordination vows.

We once knew a clergyman who remarked to a younger brother, after hearing him preach a sermon without notes, " Ah, my young man, that is fine, but what has become of that sermon? " When told that it was preached from very brief notes which he did not take into the pulpit, the older minister replied, " Oh, I am sorry to hear that! What will you do for sermons when you become as old as I am? I have kept every sermon I have preached since my ordination. The result is I have not had to write a single sermon for over twenty years." The last remark of the dear old man was obviously true in the judgment of those who had to listen to his dry and moldy utterances Sunday after Sunday. It also explained why this venerable brother never continued long in one place, notwithstanding his abundant supply of sermons.

A certain clergyman was wont, on many a public occasion, to remind his hearers that he had nineteen or twenty organizations of men and women, boys and girls, who met during the week in the parish house. " What a beehive of Christian activity the parish must be!" was the natural inference of the uninitiated, but to those who knew the facts, it seemed rather remarkable, that with so much going on day by day, the congregations should be so pitifully insignificant. On sober reflection, it is easily understood that there is not necessarily the slightest connection between a church crowded with eager worshipers, and any amount of mere machinery. Indeed, the more numerous and complicated the wheels of the machine, the less likelihood is there to be spiritual life. Somehow, there must be in the wheels the spirit of the living God. Otherwise it will be simply the noise of the rattling of the wheels.

But if the parson must be on his guard against

the dissipation of his resources on a great multitude of things calling him hither and thither, there is a like menace in such a condition for the people to whom he ministers.

We are very far from wishing to disparage the great importance of inducing as many people as possible to engage in church work. On the other hand, we have tried to show elsewhere, that it ought to be the aim of every clergyman to enlist his members in some form of Christian activity. To this end he should become familiar with the varied gifts, characteristics and aptitudes of those who make up his congregation, and assign each one to some definite department of religious service, where he will be most efficient and at the same time, contented to labor. A wise organization of all the forces of the parish is most commendable, if not absolutely necessary, in order to accomplish the best results.

We simply desire to emphasize the prime need of a spiritual motive in everything undertaken in the name of the church and the Christian fellowship. That which spoils and secularizes such activities, is that so often they are allowed to be begun, continued, and ended, without asking the blessing of God upon them, and doing them all in the name of Christ and through the grace of the Holy Spirit.

To keep our motives pure, and to work for the Master, with real joy and enthusiasm, we must cultivate the consciousness of His presence with us in all that we undertake. To this end, every organization should be encouraged to have its regular periods for corporate communion, at which services the members should come with special intention to renew at the altar their spirit of devotion and loyalty to the Master, and ask His blessing upon their particular enterprise. Then in opening and closing the meetings, however informal they may be, it is right and wholesome to have the presiding officer, man or woman, offer an appropriate form of prayer. The rector will always be delighted to supply suitable collects for that purpose.

It is an encouraging symptom to note that there is a growing tendency manifested in many directions, to recognize the spiritual side of all our work. The custom which obtains in some parishes of inducting men and boys into the choir, where they are to lead the prayers and praises of God's people, by making use of a brief but impressive public service, is a case in point. If those very responsible persons, whom the congregation has honored by electing them members of the vestry, could have the benefit of such a service, good results would surely follow. Properly considered, the office of Senior and Junior Warden, or the distinction of being chosen as a member of the vestry, is one not to be lightly esteemed. Such a responsibility ought surely to be closely associated with the sanctions and helps which belong to the discharge of religious functions of such far-reaching and important nature.

Thus it should be, with all the guilds and societies into which the constituency is divided.

The institutional church has, no doubt, come to stay. It is an entirely legitimate and natural outgrowth of a quickened spirit of social service and mutual helpfulness now abroad throughout the church. We should welcome that spirit, for it is essentially Christian. Christianity is, above all things, a social religion, and if we are loyal to our Master, we shall not fail to concern ourselves with those questions that deal with men and women in their social relations. How the vast multitudes of God's children, for whom Christ died, at home and abroad, shall be fed and clothed and educated and enabled to share with us the unspeakable riches of Christ — these questions are fundamental. The great pity is that in so many sections of the church catholic, and for so many centuries, these fundamental questions were not more generally asked and more bravely and unselfishly answered in the spirit and with the help of Christ.

The aim of this chapter, therefore, we need hardly say, has not been to decry the institutional church, but rather to recognize its enormous possibilities for good, and at the same time to point out its dangers and limitations.

The multiplied agencies of parochial activity can accomplish much, but nothing can take the

be comparatively safe. First, let him subordinate everything else to the spiritual interests of his people. Let him exalt the sacraments and prayer and the ministry of the word. Let him realize that souls must be built up and saved by spiritual means only. Secondly, let him aim to make his parish strong, not only locally, but on a world-wide scale. Keep the minds of your people constantly loyal and hospitable towards their larger obligations and privileges, diocesan and general. They are an integral part of the whole catholic body. Thirdly, let the parson remember that the church stands always and everywhere actively upon the side of high ideals in civic and political life. Every movement for the good of the community and his country and the world has a right to look to him as its advocate and champion. Lastly, as many organizations under modern conditions seem needful, let the parson cultivate the ability of managing them through good laymen, and laywomen. Never do anything yourself which you can persuade a good layman to do equally well. You will thus not only be conferring a great blessing on the layman, but also redeeming the time for some other service that you can perform. Try also to coöperate with other religious forces in the community along lines purely charitable. This kind of coöperation is not only wise and right, but by combination only, can it be well done. Clubs, reading-rooms, libraries, gymnasiums, playgrounds, and many other helpful agencies, may well be managed through such sane and kindly coöperation with the Y. M. C. A. and other religious organizations. By exercising a wise discrimination in this way, the parson will not be compelled so often, to his great sorrow, to " leave the word of God and serve tables." Of course, if he has the good fortune to have a real deacon or two, to assist him, possessed of the same spirit which animated the original seven, set apart to that office, he will be all the happier.

XVII

THE PARSON AND HIS DIOCESE

Thus far, we have laid emphasis on the importance of cultivating those qualities of heart and mind which will best equip the parson to minister most wisely to the spiritual edification of his congregation. This we have done, however, not because we think his responsibilities and interests should be confined to his own parish. It was John Wesley, a devoted priest of the Church of England, who was wont to say, " My parish is the whole world." In a very real sense, every consecrated minister of Christ should be ready to make the same declaration. The wider his outlook upon the spiritual needs of the whole world, and the keener and more intelligent his interest, beyond the limits of his own parish, the more efficient pastor will he be to his particular flock.

This principle will hold good, no matter what the ecclesiastical organization in which a man

finds himself. But in our own branch of the
Church Catholic, it is especially important to bear
it in mind. For in our church, the Diocese and
not the Parish is the essential unit of which the
whole body is composed. The parish does not
exist as an end in itself, but as a part of the diocese, and the dioceses combined constitute the
church at large.

The method of growth and development with
us is that a number of parishes are united into a
diocese, under the official supervision of a Bishop.
The parishes, large and small, are all members
of the one body, the diocese, and if one member
suffers, they all suffer, with it. Conversely the
honor and prosperity of one parish redound to
the prosperity of the whole diocese. As a matter
of fact, it has generally been found that a parish
which addresses itself with a generous devotion
to the building up of the Kingdom of God beyond
its own borders in the diocese has for its reward
the satisfaction of seeing its own spiritual interests vitalized, and all its parochial activities
quickened.

On the other hand, the parish that works and lives for itself alone is on the road to spiritual paralysis, which is the precursor of spiritual death. A narrow parochialism, just because it lacks the highest motive for effort, namely, an unselfish desire to help others, must inevitably lead to loss of spiritual interest and gradual disintegration. The universal law of spiritual growth, announced by our Lord, is that " He that seeketh his own life shall lose it, and he that loseth his life for my sake and the Gospel's, the same shall save it." This law is just as applicable to the parish as to the individual.

In order to take an intelligent interest in the work of the diocese, the parson should first of all acquaint himself with the canons by which its affairs are governed and regulated. The organization and machinery of dioceses differ more or less. He should also become familiar with the customs of the diocese, and its methods of procedure, some of which have grown up through tradition. It is obvious that a knowledge of the geography of the diocese, its material resources, its commercial life, its chief centers of population, and the various nationalities of which its people are composed, will be helpful to the parson.

Again, as the diocese may be regarded as a family, it will be to the parson's advantage, and contribute greatly to his comfort and happiness to know so far as may be the clergy and even the laity who make up the diocese. To this end he will gladly avail himself of every legitimate opportunity to meet his brethren when they gather annually at conventions or in smaller groups, and at more frequent intervals at Archdeaconry meetings, or Sunday school conventions, and other church assemblies. Christianity is a social religion and the church is a society of brethren united to accomplish certain great ends. To do whatever one can to develop the *esprit de corps* of diocesan life and work, makes for strength and is to be commended.

Speaking of the definition of a diocese, we recall an amusing incident which occurred in England on one occasion. As Bishop of Wyoming and Idaho, we were visiting a country parish in the Diocese of Norwich. When addressing the children of the Parish School, we asked them questions about the Bible and the Catechism and church doctrine and found them unusually well instructed. We then passed on to the matter of church organization. We asked them among other things what a diocese was. We reminded them that we had come to them as the Bishop of Wyoming and Idaho. "That is our Diocese," we said. "Now, children, what is a diocese?" One bright little fellow who sat on the front seat was very eager to answer our question and could with difficulty keep his seat until we could give him a chance. Turning to him at last we said, "My little man, you seem to know what a Diocese is. Please tell us." Quick as a flash, the lad arose and said, "A diocese, my Lord, is a district of land with the Bishop on top and the clergy underneath." The old Vicar remarked that he doubted whether any American boy could give a brighter answer.

In every well organized diocese, there are

likely to be certain institutions supported by the help of all the parishes; and also certain funds which are being established, not to mention the missionary obligations at home and abroad. All these are to be met in a spirit of glad and generous loyalty. The parson who has any adequate conception of his place in the diocese will at once get in touch with all these claims upon his help and sympathy, and imbue his people with the same intelligence and hearty desire to coöperate, which animate his own heart.

In these days of unusual activity, when appeals are so frequent, and the demands seem rather burdensome, the congregation naturally looks to the parson for guidance and inspiration. If his people see plainly that their minister regards these extra parochial calls upon their generosity as a hard and grievous load to carry, they are sure to agree with him, for they take their cue from him. In these matters, as is the priest, so are the people. The line of least resistance is always easy to follow. But let the parson be enthusiastically alive, not only to the duty, but the privilege of helping such worthy causes, and he will be surprised to find how quickly the people catch the contagion of his spirit, and how easily and gladly they will rise as a parish to meet their full share of responsibility in such helpful service.

Among the diocesan demands usually made upon the parish, and which the parson is expected to explain and justify to his busy people, and thus enlist their loyal coöperation, in meeting them, the following may be mentioned as illustrations.

First of all, as with us churchmen, the ancient aphorism accredited to an early father, " There is no church without a Bishop," it is obviously the first duty in every diocese to see that the Bishop is properly supported, so that he may, without anxiety, give himself wholly to the discharge of his duties, as chief shepherd of the flock.

In England, and in a few of the older American dioceses, the Bishop's salary and other diocesan expenses are provided for by the interest accruing from endowments established for that purpose. But in our own country it frequently happens that such endowments, either do not exist at all, or are not sufficiently large to meet the charges of the office. The method adopted therefore in the great majority of our American dioceses is that of assessing the parishes in amounts proportionate to their financial strength and ability to pay. This diocesan assessment is properly made a first charge against every parish. Until, with the growth of the church in wealth and power, adequate funds are provided for the Episcopal support, such an assessment will have to be paid. The readiness and spirit in which this obligation is met depend, as in everything else, appertaining to the welfare of the parish, greatly upon the attitude of the parson and his ability to make his people see the necessity as well as the duty and privilege of contributing to this obvious cause.

Then, there is in every parish the constant and never ending appeal for missions, Diocesan, and General. We use the words constant and never-ending deliberately, and not by way of stigma or reproach, still less of apology, but as a matter of just pride and Gospel privilege. The intelligent parson needs no argument to persuade him that if the time should ever come when he and his people are not called upon to spread the gospel at home and abroad, that hour would sound the death-knell of Christianity. (The church's only justification for existence is that she is the visible body of Christ, established by Him for the one purpose of propagating His message of love and salvation to all men.) Self-evident and plain as the missionary idea is on every page of the Gospel record, it is strange that in this age of Christian enlightenment, any clergyman should be found who is either ignorant of it or insensible to its appeal. This can only be explained by the fact that good men sometimes lose all sense of the proportion of the faith, and in the midst of parochial pressure and pre-occupation become blind to the main object of their sacred calling which is to be a co-worker with Christ in the great enterprise of making known to the world our Master's offer of peace and pardon. To fail in cultivating the missionary spirit among one's people, is the sure and speedy road to dismal defeat and disappointment for the parson. But it needs to be repeated often that, unless a clergyman is himself thoroughly imbued with the idea, that every converted man is a missionary, his people cannot be expected to love missions and to welcome the opportunity to contribute to them.

The method adopted by our church to secure the sum needed by any diocese for its missionary work, at home and abroad, is that known as the apportionment. This plan is a great advance on the unbusiness-like and unsystematic course which once prevailed. It is based on the fair and reasonable principle of asking every Christian to give according to his ability. In applying this principle to general missions, the great missionary society of the church, representing through its officers the whole body, assigns to each diocese, a certain sum estimated on the basis of its financial resources. This apportionment, cheerfully accepted by the diocese, is divided up among the respective parishes on a similar plan of distribution.

Thus it is with diocesan missions. If the sum apportioned to a Diocese or Parish does not seem just and equitable, it is always possible to appeal and have the amount readjusted. The whole system is voluntary and not compulsory. The wise parson, supported by the generous devotion of a well-instructed congregation, will soon be able to awaken in them a feeling of responsibility and even privilege in meeting their share of the amount needed.

The same general plan is followed in meeting all other diocesan obligations. Besides what we have mentioned, there are in many dioceses charitable institutions, such as hospitals, homes for orphan children, for aged men and women, and other charities. All these give the parson abundant opportunity to interest his people in benevolent objects whose maintenance is in entire harmony with the spirit of Him who went about doing good.

A diocese properly organized and wisely administered is thus enabled, by cultivating a spirit of solidarity and corporate loyalty, to achieve results which no single parish could think of undertaking.

It is for the results thus obtained that we appeal to the parson to cultivate in himself and his people, not only a strong diocesan consciousness, but also a keen diocesan pride.

If, under the leadership of his Bishop and his brethren, the parson is always found ready to coöperate in carrying forward every good cause, he will not only have the satisfaction of doing his duty, but will at the same time increase his own efficiency in his parish and his usefulness in the church at large.

A Bishop to whom the heavy responsibility of a large diocese is committed, soon learns that in his ecclesiastical family, there are those who, while they serve their respective parishes with all diligence and true devotion, also stand ready to work shoulder to shoulder with him in promoting every good work. In other words, he delights to discover that there are those who recognize the claims of the diocese upon them and their people as paramount.

THE END